Of churches, toothache and sheep

Selected papers from the
Norwich Historic Churches Trust
conferences
2014 and 2015

Edited by Nicholas Groves

Lasse Press

Text © the contributors
Design © Curran Publishing Services Ltd

All rights reserved. No reproduction, copy or transmission of this
publication may be made without written permission.

No portion of this publication may be reproduced, copied or transmitted
save with written permission or in accordance with the provisions of the
Copyright, Designs and Patents Act 1988, or under the terms of any licence
permitting limited copying issued by the Copyright Licensing Agency,
Saffron House, 6–10 Kirby Street, London EC1N 8TS.

Any person who does any unauthorized act in relation to this publication may be liable
to criminal prosecution and civil claims for damages.

The authors have asserted their right to be identified as the author of this work in
accordance with the Copyright, Designs and Patents Act 1988.

First published 2016
by the Lasse Press
2 St Giles Terrace, Norwich NR2 1NS, UK
www.lassepress.com
lassepress@gmail.com

ISBN-13: 978-0-9933069-2-1

Typeset in Garamond and Stone Sans by
Curran Publishing Services Ltd, Norwich, UK

Printed in the UK by Imprint Digital, Exeter.

Contents

Foreword — Brian Ayers ... v

Preface and acknowledgements — Nicholas Groves ... vii

Toothache, saints and churches in pre-Reformation Norfolk — John F. Beal ... 1

Theology to liturgy: the material culture of change in Norwich and beyond, c.1450–1640 — Victor Morgan ... 15

Norwich's Catholic chapels — Francis Young ... 49

'The sheep hath paid for all': church building and self-expression in the Late Middle Ages — Allan B. Barton ... 61

Valuations of churches in medieval Norfolk — Elizabeth Gemmill ... 73

The funeral of John Paston — Susan Curran ... 83

Index ... *107*

Foreword

Brian Ayers

The Friends of Norwich Historic Churches Trust exist to 'support Norwich's much-loved churches in a variety of ways'. Approaches to providing such support obviously centre on raising public awareness of the extraordinary wealth of surviving intramural medieval churches in the city of Norwich (30 parish churches, all listed Grade 1) and of those in the care of the Norwich Historic Churches Trust in particular (18 churches). This volume is the result of one such mechanism for public engagement: the holding of annual day conferences where the importance of the churches both to the history of the city and to its future development as a dynamic modern community in tune with its past can be explored.

It is a tribute to the conference organizers, and to the editor of this subsequent volume, that the meetings and publication are characterized by a commendable awareness that an understanding of the churches themselves cannot be obtained without consideration of their contexts. These contexts are not merely geographical and topographical, although the importance of the churches both one-to-another in local proximity and to developments elsewhere in the diocese are clear. Context also needs to be temporal, and it is a refreshing aspect of two of the following papers in particular that they illustrate the significance of change through time in different ways: Vic Morgan, in exploring changing liturgy in the medieval and Reformation periods, offers many insights into the impact, both constructive and destructive, upon the fabric of church buildings as well as seeking to examine changing meaning for those using the churches; adopting a different approach, Francis Young investigates the post-Reformation history of Roman Catholicism in Norwich, charting the slow emergence of first tolerance and subsequently acceptance by established society, and how this process was reflected in the creation of both borrowed and purpose-built structures.

A separate form of context is one which seeks to observe medieval church fabric and ecclesiastical practice elsewhere. Here the contribution of Allan Barton is particularly apposite, with his study of the Nottinghamshire church of Holme and the benefactions therein of the wool merchant John Barton who died in 1491. Barton's donations to the church not only survive well, enabling much interesting interpretation of subsequent pre-Reformation practice within the building, but are a useful reminder of the likely mindset and preparedness for richness of benefaction held by Norwich merchants. Within Norwich recorded examples of donations to the fabric are well known, but it is interesting to compare the splendid exterior of the south aisle of St Michael Coslany, the result of gifts from Gregory Clerk (father and son) and Robert Thorp, with the paucity of material evidence within the building that would have augmented their architectural donation.

Much interior church activity, however, can be implied from other sources, and two of the papers here contribute fascinating information on medieval ecclesiastical approaches to illness and death. That by John Beal explores the universal phenomenon of toothache and the attempts by the medieval church to offer some form of amelioration through faith as exemplified by devotion to St Apollonia. His survey of the surviving iconography of this now slightly obscure saint reveals sculpture, paintings and glass imagery both to memorialize the saint and, presumably, to aid supplication. Relics too were important, especially St Apollonia's teeth. Beal notes that Philip II of Spain in the 16th century was able 'to amass all 290 holy teeth from the mouth of Saint Apollonia'. As the medieval mind was able to believe 'that these were miracle-working relics that could help cure toothache, then it would not be illogical to believe that the relics could miraculously reproduce themselves'.

Then Susan Curran, in a fascinating analysis of the context of John Paston's funeral, argues persuasively that this costly affair in 1466, while clearly following due propriety (very expensively) with regard to the deceased man, was also very much concerned with the present and future status of the surviving family. The church experience of that family and others both at and after the funeral is notable; who can resist a smile when shown that the funeral accounts reveal a payment at the church of St Peter Hungate in Norwich 'To the glazier for taking out 2 panes of the church windows to let out the reek of the torches at the dirge and for soldering them back again' or nod understandingly that, notwithstanding an elaborate funeral, the more long-term issue of completing the tomb at Bromholm Priory was never achieved?

Finally, in this wonderfully diverse set of papers, there is an illuminating essay by Elizabeth Gemmill on the under-used resource of inquisitions post mortem (or IPMs) for church history. These documents, royal enquiries into estates usually (but not always) drawn up after the death of the tenant-in-chief, often contain information concerning the value of churches and so it is possible to use them to study patronage, the manner of control and even the careers of some clergy. Gemmill, however, takes matters further and shows how IPMs can suggest patterns of settlement and wealth distribution. Once again, the volume provides an essay which places churches within a context, this time that of local control and influence.

Volumes of collected papers can risk being disjointed. That fate has been avoided here through judicious initial selection of contributions to the conferences themselves and by editing which ensures that the main focus remains churches and, in particular, churches in Norwich and the Norwich diocese. The six papers here range from consideration of topographical location, through decoration, iconography and liturgy, to patronage, social function and doctrinal change. To use secular meanings of a religious words, it is both catholic in approach and enlightening.

Brian Ayers is a research fellow at the University of East Anglia and president of the Friends of the Norwich Historic Churches Trust.

Preface and acknowledgements

This volume is the partial result of the first two conferences held by the Norwich Historic Churches Trust. The Trust has been much concerned, since its inception in 1972, with drains and roofs, with decaying window mullions, and with finding suitable tenants for the 18 buildings of which it currently has care, but there is another side to this charge, and that is the custody of the history and heritage of these 18 buildings. (It has the largest portfolio of medieval churches in the city: the Church of England retains nine for worship, the Churches' Conservation Trust cares for three, and one is in private ownership.) In one sense they are no longer churches, as they have been deconsecrated, yet still they carry that heritage with them. Their life has not ceased since their last services were held, even if there have been periods of non-use, and in one sense the use of the term 'redundant church' is inaccurate. It is not a term applied to former schools, rectories, pubs and so on which have new uses (although one does wonder how many more Old Schools, Old Rectories, or Old Queen's Heads the country can stand!), and it is indicative of this that the churches keep, and are largely known by, their patronal dedications, whoever may be occupying them (even if, for example, St James Pockthorpe is better known as the Puppet Theatre). Their international importance as a collection is widely acknowledged, even if sometimes more in word than in deed. But they are more than buildings: they are foci of their parishes' histories.

An annual conference was conceived in 2014 as a means of both opening up and delving into these histories, and putting them in the widest context both locally and nationally (we await an international perspective), as well as of publicizing the Trust's work. But in order not to make the material too narrowly focused, we asked for papers on topics that deal with churches in any aspect – historical, archæological, architectural, social, art-historical, liturgical, theological – and we certainly have that breadth here: it is reflected in the title. So this volume contains papers dealing not only with the Norwich churches, but with their sisters 'out in the County' (Norfolk), as well as in Nottinghamshire, Lincolnshire and Devon; and with what some would regard as their 'original owners', the Roman Catholic Church. Speakers included academics and doctoral students, as well as independent historians, again demonstrating the wide variety of interest in churches.

The book is a 'partial result' as it was decided that, rather than publish the papers of each of the first two conferences as separate volumes, it made more sense to conflate them, and publish thematically. So another volume, which takes reuse of churches as its theme, will follow in due course.

My thanks go first to Stella Eglinton, the Trust's administrator, who assisted me with setting up the conferences, and the staff of the House of Prayer at St Edmund Fishergate, where the first one was held, and the King's Centre, where the second one took place. Brian Ayers, the president of the Friends, has not only provided a Foreword for this volume, he also chaired both conferences, and thanks are due to him for his continuing interest and support. I wish also to thank Susan Curran, a fellow trustee, for her untiring work not only in copy editing, designing and indexing the book, but in chivvying authors and editor alike so that it could be brought to completion; the authors for agreeing to give papers at the conferences and for preparing them for publication; and my colleagues on the Trust, and also the Friends' group, for agreeing to support the conferences in the first place. Finally, as a conference with no audience has failed in its object, I wish to thank those who attended to hear the papers, and contributed to the discussions after they had been read. Some of these papers have been amended in the light of these discussions.

Edward Tillett, in concluding his history *St George Tombland: Past and Present* in 1891, hoped that the subscribers would 'one and all, find something which will either interest or amuse', and it is my hope that readers of this volume will also be interested and amused.

Nicholas Groves
Norwich, April 2016

Dr Nicholas Groves is a freelance lecturer and writer in church history. His previous publications have included The Medieval Churches of the City of Norwich *and* William Stephen Gilly: An exceptionally busy life, *the biography of a 19th-century clergyman. He is a trustee of the Norwich Historic Churches Trust.*

Victor Morgan wishes to thank Carole Hill, Gudrun Warren at the Dean and Chapter Library, Norwich Cathedral, and the ever-helpful staff at the Heritage Library in Norwich. Figure 5 in his contribution is copyright the Bodleian Library, Oxford and appears with permission. Figures 1, 3, 4, 6, 7, 9, are copyright Norfolk Museums Service and appear with permission. Other photographs are by the author.

The publishers thank the Friends of the Norwich Historic Churches Trust for financial help towards the publication of this volume, all profits from which go to the Norwich Historic Churches Trust to help maintain Norwich's legacy of redundant medieval churches in the Trust's care.

The publishers also thank the Federation of Norfolk Historical and Archaeological Organisations for a grant towards the use of colour in the illustrations in this volume.

Facing page and overleaf: prints of Norwich churches from
Corbridge's map of Norwich of 1707.

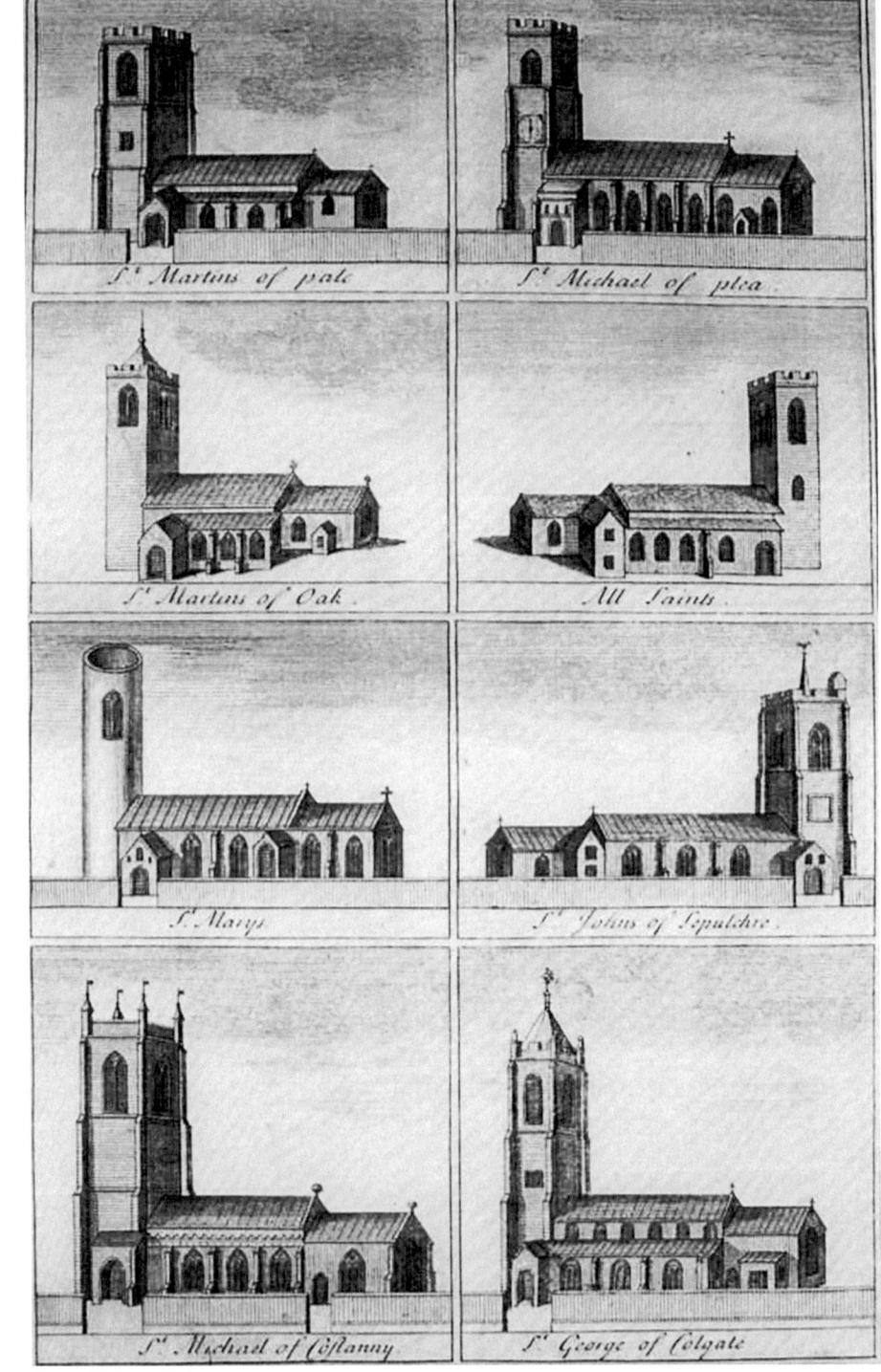

Toothache, saints and churches in Pre-reformation Norfolk

John F. Beal

The first question to ask is 'was toothache a problem in pre-reformation England?' We have archaeological information about the state of dental health from excavated skulls dating from medieval times, and can therefore assess what symptoms would have been experienced by the owners of the teeth during their lifetime. Specific evidence about the dental problems actually suffered may be obtained from letters and diaries written by royalty and wealthy people who were literate. For example, Mary Tudor, 18-year-old sister of Henry VIII, recently widowed from toothless Louis XII of France, wrote in 1515 asking Henry to allow his surgeon to stay a while longer 'for by case I am very ele bessyde of the tothe acke and mother with all, that som tym I (wit) not wat for to do'.[1]

Rich people, who could afford sugar, including honey, did suffer from tooth decay. Of Mary and Henry's father, Henry VII, it was written 'Dentes raros et exiguos, et subnigros' (His teeth few, poor and blackish). But most people had very little sugar, except that naturally occurring in fruit, and so had little decay. So why was toothache and tooth loss a common occurrence? The cause lay in a different aspect of their diet. They ate foods, such as bread made from coarsely ground flour, that were abrasive and which resulted in considerable wear on the surface of the teeth. The teeth were ground flat (which would also have made them even less susceptible to decay) and eventually the pulp (nerve) became exposed. This would have caused considerable pain, and would have often led to the pulp becoming infected and an abscess forming at the tip of the root of the tooth. In addition dental hygiene was poor and scurvy was not uncommon, especially among the rich who scorned uncooked fruit and vegetables. This led to a high prevalence of gum disease, which led in turn to the bone supporting the teeth to be affected, causing the teeth to become mobile and eventually to fall out.

It is not uncommon for stone carvings in churches to show what is generally thought to be a man with toothache. Perhaps the best known is a carving on the capital of one of the pillars in the south aisle of Wells Cathedral. Of course, we can never know exactly what was in the mind of those medieval stonemasons, but similar carvings are found in several Norfolk churches, including one of the interior label stops of the clerestory windows on the north aisle of Roughton church (Figure 1), in the south porch at North Elmham, and on a corbel of the west tower arch at Brinton. Grotesques on the exterior of Cromer and Ickburgh churches may also represent a man with toothache. In Southwold church in Suffolk a choir stall arm-rest has a carving of man with toothache, and at Norwich Cathedral one of the supporters on a misericord has a carving said to be an ape with toothache.

So what could you do if you had toothache? You could try various herbal remedies, but they were unlikely to be very effective. Perhaps a visit to the local blacksmith would enable the offending teeth to be extracted. He had a workshop, he could make the necessary tools,

Figure 1 'Man with toothache', Roughton church

he was strong, but he had no training. Maybe an itinerant toothdrawer would make an occasional visit to your village. They could often be identified by a row of teeth on their belt or in a garland round their neck. Like the blacksmith they had no training, learning their trade by trial and error. The reassurance that it would not hurt led to the saying 'He lies like a toothdrawer.' They often had a secondary occupation such as blood-letting or corn-cutting.

The earliest known toothdrawer is William le Tothdrawer, who was imprisoned in York for assault in 1301. Whether the complainant was a patient or not is unknown! An alternative in towns might be a barber, or later, a barber-surgeon. These individuals had a dwelling or shop, and undertook toothdrawing as well as shaving in addition to other operations such as bleeding. In later medieval times they had training in the form of an apprenticeship, and belonged to a trade gild (or guild) which exerted some control over who could be recognized as a barber-surgeon.

So what was the alternative? One way of seeking relief from any disease or misfortune was to invoke the prayers of one of the saints. A number of saints were believed to have powers to help with specific conditions, and one of these was St Apollonia, the patron saint of sufferers from toothache. We learn from the Legenda Aurea[2] (the Golden Legend) that she was a virgin, well along in years (although she is always depicted as an attractive young woman). It is said that she was martyred in Alexandria in AD 249 during the reign of Decenius, when the authorities were persecuting Christians for their faith. First they beat out all her teeth, then they built a huge wood pyre and told her to worship their idols or be burned alive. Apollonia broke free and threw herself into the fire, no doubt causing the church authorities a problem in determining whether she had committed suicide. It was decided that she had been led by the Holy Spirit to take this action and therefore she could be recognized as a martyred saint.

There are a number of references to prayers seeking the intercession of St Apollonia for the relief of toothache, including one which is recorded in the Commonplace Book of Robert Reynes of Acle, Norfolk (died *c.*1505).[3]

One of two paintings at the National Gallery in which St Apollonia features is of Saints Genevieve and Apollonia, painted in 1506 by Lucas Cranach the Elder. This is on the reverse of one of the shutters of his St Catherine Altarpiece. Another painting, which is of particular interest to students of medieval drama, is the *The Martyrdom of St Apollonia*, a miniature by Jean Fouquet (1452–60). It shows a dramatic rendering of her martyrdom as part of a medieval mystery play. Whether there ever was such a play is not known, but it is of great value in demonstrating how the mystery plays were performed. The picture is now in the Musée Condé, Chantilly, France.

The only known relic of St Apollonia now in existence in Norfolk is at the Shrine in Walsingham (Figure 2). There are, however, other relics said to be of the saint, one of which is in the British Dental Association Museum and another in the Victoria and Albert Museum. It is said that Philip II of Spain (who ruled from 1556–98), an avid collector of relics, managed 'to amass all 290 holy teeth from the mouth of Saint Apollonia', and Edward VI of England (ruled 1547–53), concerned about the excess of superstition, ordered all relics of St Apollonia's teeth to be handed in. Sufficient to fill a tun were collected, incorrectly sometimes described as being a ton of teeth.[4] Today we find this unbelievable and cannot understand how anyone could accept these as true relics. However, to the medieval mind, if you believed that these were miracle-working relics that could help cure toothache, then it would not be illogical to believe that the relics could miraculously reproduce themselves.

Turning to representations of St Apollonia in British churches, I have identified a total of 69 in 67 churches (two churches have two stained glass windows showing her), almost all of which date from before the Reformation. In addition there are known to be at least a further five representations no longer in existence. Of these almost half are painted on rood screens (30) and most of the rest are in stained glass windows (32). Four are carved in stone, one is in a wall painting and one is a tapestry. Approximately one-third of these

Figure 2
Tooth relic of St Apollonia at the Anglican shrine, Walsingham

representations are in East Anglia, another third in Devon, while the remaining third are scattered across the country, but none north of Bunbury in Cheshire. In addition there is one bell dedicated to St Apollonia.

There are 16 churches in Norfolk that are known to have had representations of St Apollonia. As in Britain as a whole, half of them are on rood screen panels (10), seven in stained glass and two carved in stone. Eamon Duffy has analysed the figures painted on rood screens in East Anglia and Devon, the two areas of the country in which the majority of painted screens remain. Excluding the most important saints, namely the Blessed Virgin Mary, the Apostles, the four Evangelists and the four Doctors of the church, St Apollonia is the fifth most frequently represented saint, and in Devon she is the most frequently depicted saint.[5]

Norfolk churches in which St Apollonia may be seen on rood screen panels are at Barton Turf (Figure 3), one of the finest rood screens in England; Horsham St Faith, Ludham, Dersingham, Wolferton (much damaged) and Binham. In the latter the panels were over-painted in white, on top of which texts from Cranmer's Bible of 1539 were written in Black Letter script, probably in the 1560s, early in the reign of Elizabeth I. The rood screen is no longer in place but several of the panels are on display in the church. The covering paint is now wearing thin and in places some of the saints can be seen showing through. Behind the text for 1 Timothy 6 v. 6–9 a saint is visible, below which the top part of the name Apollonia can be seen.

Two other panels still exist but are not now in the churches. The panel from Lessingham, said to be from one of the rood screen doors, was for a time on display in St Peter Hungate church in Norwich. It is now in the care of the Norfolk Museums Service and is in storage at their Gressenhall facility, although it does not yet feature in their online catalogue. A single panel from St Augustine's Norwich has recently been restored and is now on display at St Peter Hungate. There was at one time a panel in Babingley church, now a ruin, on which St Apollonia was depicted. A small painting of the panel is held by the British Library. Finally, the church at Thorpe-next-Haddiscoe is known to have had a panel depicting St Apollonia although it is no longer extant. This is evidenced by an entry in Thomas Martin's 18th-century 'Norfolk Collections' in which he states that the panel shows a saint 'with a pair of pincers' and provides a small drawing showing a pair of pincers containing a tooth (NRO Rye 17 Vol 2 folio 181).

This list cannot end without describing a rood screen panel in a church in Suffolk, although it is in the Diocese of Norwich. This is at Somerleyton, where St Apollonia is shown holding a hammer used to remove her teeth and a book on which her extracted teeth are lying. This is the only such representation known to the author.

Turning to St Apollonia shown in stained glass, there are two such representations in Norwich. The first is in the south aisle of Norwich Cathedral, where a roundel shows the saint holding an extremely large pair of pincers. The second is in the tracery of the East window of St Stephen's church (Figure 4). Another roundel was at one time on display in St Peter Hungate and is now said to be in the store of the Norfolk Museums Service. Two other Norfolk churches, Cley and Sandringham, have stained glass tracery windows of St Apollonia. There is a further possible former representation in stained glass in the church at Stiffkey. In the south aisle there is a window with many fragments of medieval stained glass. One of the pieces shows a hand holding a pair of pincers although it is unclear

Figure 3 St Apollonia on a rood screen panel at Barton Turf

what the pincers contain between their claws. The possibility that the window originally depicted St Agatha cannot be ruled out entirely, as she is sometimes shown holding pincers containing a breast, but this would not be her usual attribute, especially in this area, and it is most likely to have been part of a St Apollonia window.

The two representations of St Apollonia carved in stone are on the Erpingham Gate at Norwich Cathedral (Figure 5) and at Docking on the pedestal of the font.

Undoubtedly a number of churches would have had other images of St Apollonia, but no record of these remains in most cases. One exception is at Hingham, where it is known that there were 28 images in the church, of which St Apollonia was one.[6] Each of these images had a light, either a wax taper or candle, which was kept burning during Divine Service. In addition Blomefield reports that the sacrist at Norwich Cathedral reported in the accounts offerings 'at St Appolonia' but whether this was an image or an altar dedicated to the saint in the cathedral is not clear.[7]

Many medieval vestments had saints embroidered on the orphrey, of which a few are still in existence. I am not aware of any depicting St Apollonia which survive in Norfolk; the nearest is a 15th-century English cope at Ely Cathedral on which the saint is embroidered.

Clearly St Apollonia was an important saint for the wealthier members of the community in medieval society. It was they who paid for, or made donations towards, church

Figure 4 St Apollonia in stained glass, St Stephen's, Norwich

furnishings such as rood screens and stained glass windows, and they would have had a say on which saints were depicted. There are further indications of her importance to well-off members of medieval society. Anne Boleyn's paternal grandfather Sir William Boleyn (1451–1505), a wealthy mercer and Lord Mayor of London, in his will called upon a list of 19 saints whose prayers he sought. One of these was St Apollonia. We are left to wonder whether he had had recourse during his life to invoking St Apollonia for the relief of toothache. The site of the tomb of Sir William Boleyn (or Bullen) may be seen on the south side of the chancel in Norwich Cathedral, surrounded by paintings of the family coat of arms depicting three bull's heads. There are also several instances of St Apollonia being associated with royalty. Richard Duke of Gloucester (later Richard III), in the Statutes for the establishment of a college of canons at Middleham, named her as one of the saints to whom he had a special devotion. She is one of the saints carved in stone in the Henry VII Chapel at Westminster Abbey, and she is also found on the outside wall of the Chantry Chapel of Prince Arthur (Henry VIII's older brother) in Worcester Cathedral.

In medieval England every town had a number of gilds, and many villages had one or more. Each gild was dedicated to a particular saint. Every gild was required by Parliament in 1389 to submit a return setting out details of the gild ordinances and properties. Some of the returns have survived and are now kept at the National Archives. Details of others are known from wills, court rolls and other medieval documents. St Apollonia was not the dedication saint of many gilds, but of the few that were dedicated to her, one was in Lynn. The gild of St Apollonia is listed in the town's Account Roll for 1371–2, as during this period every gild was required to pay a levy based on their wealth towards repairing the dykes around the town and making good the defences.

Figure 5 St Apollonia carved in stone on Erpingham Gate, Norwich Cathedral

While St Apollonia was the saint most frequently associated with relief from toothache, she was not the only saint for whom there is reliable contemporary evidence of being invoked for this purpose. Mention will be made of three with a specific Norfolk connection. The first of these is St Æthelthryth, better known as St Etheldreda or St Audrey (c.636–679), the founder and abbess of a monastery at Ely, later to become Ely Cathedral. At Thetford, in Norfolk, a church dedicated to St Etheldreda (or St Audrey) had a precious relic – her smock. This relic was much sought after by pilgrims seeking 'putting away the Toth-ach,

and the swelling of the Throte'.[9] This church and its relics were all destroyed at the Reformation. Other relics of the saint still exist at St Etheldreda's RC Church, Ely and St Etheldreda's RC Church, Ely Place, Holborn, London. A dozen medieval churches dedicated to St Etheldreda still exist, one of which, in King Street, is in the care of the Norwich Historic Churches Trust.

There are several representations of her in Norfolk, in which she is often depicted holding a model of Ely Cathedral. She may be seen on the opposite side to the St Apollonia carving on the arch at Erpingham Gate, Norwich Cathedral, in a modern stained glass window at St Peter Mancroft, Norwich, on one of the marvellous rood screen panels at Ranworth church, and also on the rood screen at Gateley (Figure 6), in stained glass at the wonderful Salle church, and carved on the pedestal of the font from St James, Pockthorpe, Norwich (now in the church of St Mary Magdalene).

Another of the saints for whom there is a record of curing toothache is St William of Norwich. A biography of this saint can be found in 'The Life and Miracles of St William of Norwich by Thomas of Monmouth'.[10] William was born in 1132 and was baptised by the parish priest of Haveringland. It is thus usually assumed that he grew up in Haveringland. His father died when he was young and when he was eight he left home to become apprenticed to a peltier

Figure 6 St Etheldreda on a rood screen panel at Gateley

(skinner). On one of his visits home, when he was 12 years old, a man came to the house and offered him a post in the kitchen of the archdeacon in Norwich, which would provide a good education and set him up for life. Although his mother resisted, the man insisted and gave William's mother three pieces of silver to persuade her to allow William to go.

There is a stained glass window now in the Victoria and Albert Museum, which is identified as originating from the Norwich School of glass making. It has been suggested it might show William going away with the man and saying goodbye to his mother.[11] Two days later he was dead. His body was taken to, and hidden in, Thorpe Wood, now part of Mousehold Heath on the outskirts of Norwich. When it was found it was at first buried where it lay, but later it seems to have been moved to a chapel in the wood which was later dedicated as the Chapel of St William, the site of which can still be seen on Mousehold Heath.

Claims were made that this was a ritual murder of a Christian boy carried out by the Jews at the time of Passover. However, Anderson has examined all the evidence in detail and shown conclusively that William was not killed by the Jews, and that this claim was part of an anti-Semitic pattern of alleged ritual murders.[12] Later William's remains were moved to the monks' cemetery at Norwich Cathedral, where it was increasingly venerated as a relic of a holy martyr. As Norwich Cathedral did not have a shrine which would attract pilgrims and their money, three further translations were made when the relics were moved to more important positions within the precincts, initially to the Chapter House and thence into the church, first on the south side of the high altar and finally to the north side. Thomas of Monmouth, one of the monks at the Cathedral, became the leading promoter of William's shrine and recorded the miracles that took place there. Two of these concerned pilgrims suffering from toothache, both of whom were cured at William's tomb. The first was 'de quodam clerico a dolore dentium liberato' (a certain cleric cured of toothache) and the second 'de monacho a dolore consimili curato' (a monk cured of a similar pain).

Although he was never formally canonized, St William became a popular saint for a time in Norfolk, but not more widely. The church at William's home parish of Haveringland has three bells, one of which is the only bell in existence, and probably the only one ever made, dedicated to St William. There are five (possibly six) rood screens depicting St William of Norwich. The screen at Loddon is of interest because instead of the more usual single panels with paintings of individual saints, it has double panels showing biblical and other scenes. One of these double panels shows St William being martyred by being nailed to a transverse pole across two uprights (Figure 7). On one of the rood screen panels at Worstead, St William is represented wearing a crown of thorns and holding two nails representing his alleged martyrdom, at Litcham he holds three nails in his left hand and a knife in his right, and on the screen at Eye in Suffolk he is shown with his hands and feet pierced and holding a large cross and three nails. A rood screen from St John Maddermarket, and now at the Victoria and Albert Museum, depicts St William holding nails in his right hand and a knife in his left. In St Mary Magdalene church in Norwich there is a rood screen panel which was originally in St James, Pockthorpe, and which has a painting said by some to show St William holding a peltier's knife. In the Norwich church of St Julian the base of the font has a carved figure of St William holding a peltier's knife. Another font pedestal which shows St William being martyred is seen at Great

Figure 7 St William of Norwich on a rood screen panels at Loddon

Witchingham. This font is of interest as it still has some of its medieval paintwork. There was a wall painting at Ashby, Suffolk said to include St William, but this had been covered with whitewash when Keyser wrote his monumental list of buildings in Great Britain and Ireland having mural and other painted decorations, published in 1883.[13]

There were at least five gilds in Norfolk dedicated to St William of Norwich. Three of these were in Norwich, one of which was the Peltiers Gild of the Holy Trinity and the Holy Innocent St William the Martyr based at the Cathedral, one at St Michael Berstreet, and one at the church of the Dominican Friars (Blackfriars). The other two were at Haveringland[14] and the Young Scholars Gild at Lynn.[15] It is known that there was an altar and light dedicated to St William at St Michael Coslany, Norwich.[16]

The fourth saint with specific connections to Norfolk is Master (or Sir) John

S(c)horn(e). Like St William of Norwich, Master John Schorn was never canonized – that is, he was never officially recognised as a saint by the wider church – but was a 'local' or 'popular saint' treated as a saint by general acclaim. However, as we shall see, veneration of him became much more widespread than that of St William. The alternative title of 'Sir' is not an indication that he was knighted, but was a title commonly given to priests, rather like the present day title of 'Father', often if they did not hold a university degree. Most depictions of John Schorn show him in the robes of a Doctor of Divinity, so the title of 'Master' or 'Magister' implying that he had a degree is probably correct.

Little is known about the early life of John Schorn. It is thought that he may have been a monk at Christchurch Canterbury (now Canterbury Cathedral) and he may have studied at Oxford University. By 1273 he seems to have been connected to the Augustinian Priory at Dunstable. In $c.1289$ a John de Schorne was appointed by the Archbishop of Canterbury as rector of Monks Risborough, Buckinghamshire, but it is not known whether this was the same John Schorn. However, it is known that in 1290 he was appointed as rector of North Marston, Buckinghamshire, the advowson of which was held by Dunstable Priory. He remained rector of that parish until his death in 1314. In his will he directed that his body should be buried before the high altar at North Marston Church.

Schorn had a reputation as a very holy man, and it was said that he had horny knees from many hours of praying daily. He also had a reputation for curing gout, and it is thought that he developed an audio-visual aid to demonstrate this by making a boot into which he conjured the devil, or perhaps he conjured the devil out of it, an early form of Jack-in-the-Box. It is also said that during a drought he struck his staff into the ground, whereupon water gushed out leading to a perpetual spring. The water was claimed to have healing properties. The well over the spring still exists at North Marston, and has recently been renovated. Unlike many local saints, devotion to Master John Schorn was not only geographically widely spread but also had a long-lasting popularity, continuing right up to the Reformation. His body was buried in North Marston church and it is known that the east window of the church had stained glass depicting him until at least 1660. Pilgrims flocked to his tomb at North Marston, and many miracles are claimed to have followed, especially cures of gout and ague, but also of eye afflictions. It is also recorded that he brought two drowned boys back to life and restored life to some dead cattle.

In 1480 Richard Beauchamp, Bishop of Salisbury and Dean of St George's Chapel, Windsor, petitioned Pope Sixtus IV to transfer the shrine of John Schorn from North Marston to St George's Chapel. When John Schorn was removed an image, probably made of wood, was placed in North Marston church, and this itself became a 'miracle-working' image. The resultant pilgrim donations led to continuing elaborate embellishment of the church building. Meanwhile pilgrims started to visit his shrine at St George's Chapel, Windsor. In 1484, by order of King Richard III, the bones of King Henry VI were transferred from Chertsey Abbey to Windsor, thus increasing the pilgrim traffic. The pilgrim money box for King Henry is still in St George's Chapel, and although the box for pilgrim offerings at John Schorn's shrine no longer survives, the bill for making the box exists in the College Archives. At least two designs of pilgrim badges from the period have been found, one of him preaching in a pulpit by the side of which is a boot, and the other of him standing holding a large boot out of which a devil is poking.

It is known from a letter written by Cardinal Thomas Wolsey in 1521 that King Henry VIII intended to make a pilgrimage to the shrine of John Schorn in gratitude for his recovery from a fever.[17] Whether he actually made the pilgrimage is not known. There are also wills that mention pilgrimage to Master John Schorn. It was not unusual for those who had intended to make pilgrimages to holy sites, but had not actually made them, to leave money in their will to pay others to do it for them after their death, in order for the testator to gain remission from time in purgatory. One such will was that of John Tyzard of Cratfield, Suffolk in 1483. He bequeathed 13s 4d for a man to go on pilgrimage to Canterbury, to Master John Schorn, to Woolpit [our Lady] and to Walsingham. Another was the 1510 will of Robert Harryes of Ticehurst, Sussex, in which he left Robert Hope and John Bele 26s 8d 'to make pilgrimages to the Blessed Mary of Walsingham, St Thomas the Martyr of Canterbury, to the blood of the Lord Jesus at Hailes and Master John Schorne'. It is clear that the Schorn's shrine was perceived as being of major importance, a conclusion confirmed by the fact that the reformist bishop of Worcester, Hugh Latimer, in one of his published sermons railing against 'popish pilgrimage', specifically mentioned pilgrimage to 'Mr John Shorn' and to 'our Lady of Walsingham' in his attack.

There are three rood screens in Norfolk on which there are paintings of Master John Schorn. These are at Cawston, Gateley (Figure 8: detail showing Master John Schorn holding a boot out of the top of which a devil appears) and Suffield. In addition to the surviving paintings of Master John Schorn on these rood screens, there is evidence that there was an image of John Schorn at Binham Priory. In the will of Richard Esyngwold, gentleman of Islip, Northamptonshire, proved in the Prerogative Court of Canterbury in 1508, it states that he requests 'my body to be buried in the Abbey church of Bynham before the holy ymage of master John Shorn'. There is also one rood screen depicting John Schorn at Sudbury, Suffolk and there are three (possibly four) in Devon.

But what about toothache? In the archives of St George's Chapel, Windsor is an illuminated manuscript which was written *c*.1430–50 and is known as the *Schorn Book of Hours*.[18] Inside the back of this book is a handwritten hymn that may have been used by pilgrims to the shrine. There is also a similar copy of the hymn at the British Library. The hymn has a number of verses extolling the miracles and deeds attributed to Master John Schorn. One verse reads:

> Hail, help of the sick / medicine of those harassed / by the pain of fevers
> Hail, light of the eyes / liberator of the weak / from the toothache
> Hail, since the ox / restored to life / gives witness of your miracles
> Hail, thou who art the / rescuer of all the drowned / by thy prayers…

Clearly the relief of toothache was one of the miracles attributed to Master John Schorn.

Dr John Beal *is a retired dentist who was regional consultant in dental public health for Yorkshire and the Humber. He continues to hold an honorary senior lectureship in dental public health at the University of Leeds. He has an interest in dental history and medieval church history, especially the cult of saints. He brings these together in his research, of which this chapter is a part. He is a past chairman of the Lindsay Society for the History of Dentistry and a former member of the Church Buildings Council.*

TOOTHACHE, SAINTS AND CHURCHES 13

Figure 8 Detail from image of Master John Schorn on a rood screen panel at Gateley

Notes

1. *Letters and Papers, Foreign and Domestic, Henry VIII*, Vol. 2, 1515–1518, ed. J. S. Brewer, HMSO, London, 1864, pp. 11–30. www.british-history.ac.uk/letters-papers-hen8/vol2/pp11-30 (accessed 18 December 2014).
2. Jacobus De Voragine (c.1260) *Legenda Aurea.*
3. Bodleian Library, Oxford, MS. Tanner 407, Commonplace book of Robert Reynys of Acle, Norfolk (c.1470).
4. Chemnicio, Martino (Chemnitius, Martinus) (1584) Examinis Concilii Tridentini, https://play.google.com/books/reader?id=DrtEAAAAcAAJ&printsec=frontcover&output=reader&hl=en&pg=GBS.PP1 (accessed 18 December 2014).
5. Duffy, E. (1990) 'Holy maydens, holy wyfes: the cult of women saints in fifteenth- and sixteenth-century England', pp. 175–96 in W. J. Shiels and D. Wood (eds), *Women in the Church* (Studies in Church History, vol. 27), Blackwell, Oxford.
6. Upcher, A. C. W. (1921) History of Hingham, Norfolk, and its church of St. Andrew, https://archive.org/details/historyofhingham00upch (accessed 18 December 2014).
7. Blomefield, F (1805) *An essay towards a Topographical History of the County of Norfolk*, Vol 4, pp. 40–1. https://archive.org/details/essaytowardstopo04blom (accessed 18 December 2014).
8. Hillen, H. J. (1912) *History of the Borough of King's Lynn.*
9. Blomefield, F. (1805) *Towards a Topographical History of the County of Norfolk*, Vol. 2, pp. 59–76, www.british-history.ac.uk/topographical-hist-norfolk/vol2/pp59-76 (accessed 18 December 2014).
10. Jessop, A. and James, M. R. (trans.) (1896) *The Life and Miracles of St William of Norwich by Thomas of Monmouth.*
11. Personal communication from T. Bloxham (2013) Victoria and Albert Museum, relating to tentative identification by Christopher Woodforde in 1946.
12. Anderson, M. D. (1964) *A Saint at Stake*, Faber & Faber, London.
13. Keyser, C. E. (1883) *A list of buildings in Great Britain and Ireland having mural and other painted decorations, of dates prior to the latter part of the sixteenth century, with historical introduction and alphabetical index of subjects*, https://ia601403.us.archive.org/4/items/listofbuildingsi00soutiala/listofbuildingsi00soutiala.pdf (accessed 18 December 2014).
14. Blomefield, F. (1808) *Towards A Topographical History of the County of Norfolk*, Vol. 8, pp. 226–34, www.british-history.ac.uk/topographical-hist-norfolk/vol8/pp226-234 (accessed 18 December 2014).
15. Toulmin Smith, J. (1870) *English Gilds: The Original Ordinances of More than One Hundred Early English Gilds*, Early English Text Society/Oxford University Press, London.
16. Blomefield, F. (1806) *Towards A Topographical History of the County of Norfolk*, Vol. 4, Part II, pp. 479–503, www.british-history.ac.uk/topographical-hist-norfolk/vol4/pp479-503 (accessed 18 December 2014).
17. Brewer, J. S. (ed.) (1867) *Letters and Papers, Foreign and Domestic, Henry VIII, Vol 3, 1519–1523*, HMSO, London, pp. 485–516, www.british-history.ac.uk/letters-papers-hen8/vol3/pp485-516 (accessed 18 December 2014).
18. www.stgeorges-windsor.org/archives/archive-features/image-of-the-month/title1/schorn-book-of-hours.html (accessed 18 December 2014).

Theology to liturgy: the material culture of change in Norwich and beyond, c.1450–1640[1]

Victor Morgan

Introduction

This is a preliminary foray into sketching out some of the ways in which the material form of religious buildings and objects can be used as a point of entry to understanding the changing spiritual concerns of the past. Both historically and contemporaneously we endow all sorts of object with meaning, albeit our meanings may differ. Quite ordinary objects are imbued with and communicate values and beliefs, which may be specific to an individual or shared among a wider community.[2]

Religious buildings and objects are a special case because from their outset they are *consciously* symbolic in the minds of their creators and users. Because they usually arise from shared endeavour and almost invariably involve communal use, they can tell us things about widely held values and beliefs in the past. However pre-modern attitudes towards all objects were fundamentally different from those that prevail in our consumerist society. Practically everything had a symbolic meaning and in various ways represented something that was immaterial. The demarcation between the material and the ethereal was not what it was to become from the Enlightenment onwards. Even after the Reformation God was seen to be immanent in the world, intervening at times in the circumstances of human existence. This was a very different view of the world from the one that prevails today, and it requires an effort of the historical imagination to grasp it. My experience in trying to teach this sort of thing is that material objects, when themselves properly explained, can help towards this process of understanding, lending an immediacy to the abstract.

My main focus is on the period 1450–1640, and on Norwich's city churches, although at points I range beyond them into the historic diocese of Norwich.[3]

The Norwich legacy

My core argument is that ultimately for the great majority of our ancestors abstract theological ideas were experienced through the material practices of the liturgy and understood through that experience. Sometimes they elaborated on that experience. However 'reading' the surviving material culture can be difficult, for two main reasons. First, what survives today is not a true measure of what once was. Norwich retains only a tiny fraction of the homes of common people in the early modern period, but a much higher proportion of the great houses of the period survive in some form.[4] Something similar is true of ecclesiastical buildings, although the pattern is rather different.

Norwich is unusual in retaining not only a former monastic cathedral but a transmogrified Great Hospital and substantial parts of a former friary. But this is but a denuded residue of the rich diversity of religious establishments that once populated the late-medieval city. This included the enclaves within the walls of the four great friaries which supplemented the parish churches in serving the city's spiritual needs. The Blackfriars church remains (as St Andrews and Blackfriars Halls), as do parts of the associated building complex. In addition (but with hardly anything remaining today) there were the Whitefriars across the river in the area now occupied by a site currently being redeveloped by Jarrolds. Downstream, along the line of the river, and between the river and King Street, were first the Greyfriars and then the Austin friars.

These imparted a quite different sense to the organization of the urban landscape than now we experience. For example, the outer wall of the Greyfriars, fragments of which survive to this day, ran in parallel and close proximity to the wall of the Cathedral Close, with only a narrow lane between them. Recent demolition and redevelopment – or lack of redevelopment – has provided an opportunity to capture a sense of the scale of these enclaves.

Around the city's walls were minor hospitals and chapelries. At Carrow a priory provided a convenient 'parking lot' for the surplus daughters of the county's gentry and the city's elite. At the heart of the city were what might be described as great 'prayer factories', which today survive only in changed form or not at all. St Peter Mancroft sustained so many chantry priests that the incumbent was known as 'the prior of Mancroft'. Across the road was the secular college of St Mary in the Fields. Here not only individuals but also many guilds had their chantry chapels, and it was evidently the focus for much pre-Reformation civic ceremony. In addition, recent work suggests that almost all the religious houses of the county maintained town houses in Norwich. Today, none of these survive in a recognizable form.

The city also hosted anchors and hermits – mystical recluses, sometimes attached to churches, as with Julian, and sometimes stashed away over the city gates. Fragmentary evidence suggests it also may have supported three beguinages, avowed communities of female laity, although in forms less developed than existed just across the North Sea. Everywhere this was a distinctly urban phenomenon.[5]

While these lay communities may not have had a long life, their fleeting presence tells us something about the aspirations of late medieval lay religiosity. The model was ascetic: of renunciation, living out within the world the life of Christ. In some respects the beguines shared common ground with anchorites and hermits. Often there was mystical inspiration fired by intense piety and – disconcertingly for authority – claiming a direct relationship with God. Again, this was personal and individualistic. These were practitioners of the religion of the spirit as against the prevailing religion of authority. Could it be that this was a reaction to the emphasis on the multiplying ritual practices that were most fully realizable in a large and wealthy city? The social underclass in Norwich might also have provided a focus for organized charitable activity that was not feasible in rural parishes. At the same time the movement shared at least one aspect of the elaborated religiosity to which it may have been a reaction: a renewed emphasis on Christ's sufferings, made real on the streets of Norwich.

So Norwich was a diversely ecclesiastical and religious city around 1500, and the buildings that survive are not always adequate evidence of what once was. The happenstance of survival of material evidence can skew our view; we need to interpret what does survive (primarily, parish churches) in the light of our knowledge of the wider ecclesiastical and religious environment of the era.

Material change and cultural change

The second problem with using the surviving material culture as a means of interpreting the past is that if buildings survive, they do so because they change. I once divided the surviving great houses of Norfolk into 'palimpsests' (whose layout and uses have changed over the years) and 'time capsules' (often run by the National Trust).[6] This problem is even more acute for parish churches.

In great houses, fashion and changing social attitudes (for instance, to privacy) led to the great hall being abandoned for the great chamber and the enfilade being replaced by the corridor. In parish churches, the appearance and precise organization of internal space was always charged with intense and self-conscious meaningfulness. Certainly in the 16th century they became battlegrounds for competing theologies expressed through alternative liturgies. A peculiar feature of the north European Reformation is that it involved the takeover of existing buildings – which had often been rebuilt in the 15th century – and the conversion of their interiors to new practices.[7] This contrasts with the somewhat later response to the Reformation by Continental post-Tridentine Catholicism, which often involved the wholesale rebuilding of churches in a manner designed through baroque emotionalism to wrest hearts and minds from its opponents.

In Norfolk in the 15th century, through to the 1540s and even somewhat later – for St Stephen's to 1550[8] – all or parts of old churches were demolished, and new and more splendid buildings rose in their place. Earlier rebuilds were characterized by the addition of aisles; this era largely saw the construction of towers and porches.[9] Both old and new buildings also saw embellishment by further decoration or the addition of new fittings. For example, much of the older seating now found in churches dates from this period, whereas before the mid-15th century the congregation had either milled around or sat on a few stone bench seats built into the walls.

This may have reflected a desire for better-defined social ordering within the church, as well as the new emphasis on preaching – a phenomenon of the pre-Reformation no less than the post-Reformation period. In Norwich and similar cities, the laity had access to a range of preachers from amongst the four mendicant orders, the monks at the cathedral and at least some of the secular clergy.

There is a single surviving inventory of a secular Norwich priest: John Baker, rector of St John Maddermarket and All Saints, Ber Street, who died in 1518. Sermons formed a substantial part of his library.[10] Richard Caister, vicar of St Stephen's from 1402 until his death in 1420, had such a reputation as a preacher that his tomb became a place of pilgrimage. A surviving pilgrim badge depicts him in the pulpit accompanied by a dove, the symbol of the Holy Spirit.[11] However, this new late-medieval emphasis on preaching may have been a more urban than rural phenomenon, despite the pulpits still to be seen in the county: there are very fine late-medieval examples at Salle, Horsham St Faith, Burnham Norton, South Burlingham, Burlingham St Edmund, St James Castle Acre and Cawston.

All save one of the seven churches along St Benedict's Street in Norwich were rebuilt in the 15th century in a manner that accommodated large congregations and preaching. Some sense of the size of the congregations that the friars attracted can be seen in the vast scale of the nave of their surviving church in Norwich.

We need to recognize that this rebuilding and refitting was also driven by changing fashions in religious beliefs and practices. It is easy, but entirely wrong, to think of medieval religious practice as unchanging. It most certainly was not. For instance, the development of the idea of purgatory and the complex culture of intercession to which it gave rise left its mark, and we can still see some evidence for it today.

Patronage and ownership

The great rebuilding of parochial churches during the (long) 15th century also saw changes in patterns of patronage. I am no expert in this area, and conceivably changes in the nature of the sources have created a distorted picture, but my sense is that a lot of this effort was funded by wealthy nobility and gentry in the countryside, and wealthy merchants in towns. The characteristic late-medieval addition of a church porch made it possible to show the family affiliations of the donors through ostentatious displays of heraldry. This may contrast with earlier periods when both impetus and resources had come rather more from the community as a whole. I would argue that the appropriation of churches for their own purposes by the gentry is a defining feature of the post-Reformation period, but this 'gentrification' was already in train, albeit in a rather different form and for quite different purposes, well before the Reformation in the 1530s to 1550s.

In the county there are the shields of the de la Poles and Wingfields on the frieze of the porch of St Agnes, Cawston,[12] and their arms on nearby Salle. Salle also has a heraldic frieze above the west doorway of the tower (c.1405–20), which combines Christian symbols with the arms of the Brews, Mauteby, Morley and Kerdiston families.[13] The south aisle and transept carry the arms of John Brigg.[14] At a time when provincial England was governed directly by great magnates or their clients, ostentatious and heraldically 'logoed' buildings blazoned forth the extent of their 'countries' or territories. It is in this context that we need to read houses such as East Barsham Hall and the architecturally associated house, later a rectory, at Great Snoring.[15] Parish churches were a rather less expensive way of achieving a similar effect. The Veres did this on a group of churches around their home at Castle Hedingham on the Suffolk–Essex border. Investment in churches also contributed to the spiritual treasury of merits of those thus memorialized.

At a more modest level this is to be seen in the funeral pall of John Westgate, alderman, with its merchant's mark – the mercantile equivalent of the gentry's arms – and the request for prayers for him and his wife.[16] At all social levels we should not underestimate the degree of personal and family proprietorialism engendered by this type of investment. It is to be read in the terms used by Roger Martyn of Long Melford in Suffolk when he refers to the Clopton chapel – still to be seen today, with its mezzanine bunk for the family's chantry priest: domestic indeed – and his own family's investment in the Jesus chapel.[17] So when the Reformation came, among other things it affronted a sense of personal property that had been developing around parish churches over at least 150 years.

Statistics on the rebuilding in Norwich pose problems, so I shall not include them here. But the general picture across the county is of widespread rebuilding and refurbishment of most parish churches from the 1470s to the 1520s.[18] In Norwich this period also saw the amalgamation of some parishes and the loss of churches that became redundant as a result. The peak of around 60 Norwich churches during the High Middle Ages fell by the 1520s to around 46, serving on average 200 to 250 parishioners.[19] Quite simply, the increasingly complex round of liturgy and multiplicity of devotions could not have been accommodated in the larger number of older but smaller churches.

If the century or more up to the Reformation is one of great parochial rebuilding, the contrast is all the more stark with the 150 years that followed, when there was practically no new building or rebuilding. Instead there were radical alterations in fitments to bring them into line with a series of doctrinal changes. So there is a paradox when we contemplate the evidence for the Reformation: this great religious watershed was not matched in the architectural record. Clearly rebuilding as distinct from reordering was not seen as a priority: what did not offend was tolerated, or its earlier meaning simply forgotten over the years.

Material reality and theological change

Let me now try to marry up these physical residues to changing theological and liturgical realities. First I should clarify my terms (in a sketchy way which I hope will not offend theologians). Essentially, in this period, theological debate was meant to be reserved for those deemed qualified to enter into it. Theological debate is resolved into doctrine. In turn, doctrine is distilled into not-to-be controverted dogma. That is, dogma is intended to be accepted by all, and is enforced by the discipline of the church which, *in extremis*, has behind it the power of the state. Finally, both doctrine and dogma are expressed in the liturgy, the form and formulary according to which public worship is conducted. Beyond the public aspect of worship there were also attempts to regulate the private devotions that became a feature of the 15th century and beyond. All this worship occurs within a material place that is organized in certain ways and accompanied by the use of designated objects. Thus, while religion may deal with the spiritual, the numinous, it is also deeply implicated in the signifying materiality of the world.

Let me make two points here which I feel are too rarely acknowledged. First, there are great similarities in the preoccupations of catholic and protestant theologians of this period. Essentially both were concerned with soteriology, the theology of salvation. Their differences were over how to achieve it. This is not and had not always been the central concern of theological debate. For instance, the Lollards from the mid-14th century onwards criticized primarily the material preoccupations of the Church: the nature of the sacraments, the corrupting effects of the Church's wealth, the veneration of objects – themes picked up by protestant reformers.[20] Today, except on the extreme fringes, we do not hear much about hellfire, purgatory or predestination. In the Church's first 200 years it appears to have been preoccupied with the nature of Christ, not the precise means of salvation. Therefore, from a longer perspective, the bitterness of dispute in this period was not the consequence of different concerns, but of shared concerns.

Second, we can overemphasize the degree of change brought about by the Reformation in England. True, much that was concrete was lost, but a shared set of common presumptions is apparent both before and after it. Today we are familiar with differences between distinct modalities of thinking, not least between radical Islamists and Westerners, but in the 16th century it was essentially a dispute within a shared – in the precise sense, preconceived – mode of thought.

Recently it has been suggested that the debate on salvation and purgatory underlies *Hamlet*,[21] not least because in Shakespeare's day it remained a preoccupation. The same was true with regard to common usage, everyday experience and material culture: much survived from the catholic past.

Protestant Englishmen were familiar with the forms and objects of the catholicism that remained in a self-consciously competitive parallel. For instance, the quarter days continued to be called Lady Day and Michaelmas. Norwich still had inns whose names had catholic significance, such as the Cardinal's Hat and the Lamb. Indeed, new markers derived from post-Tridentine catholicism were introduced, such as 'Bellarmine jar'. It is not clear how conscious people were of the catholic overtones. In parish churches there may have been a degree of archaeological amnesia or simple indifference. If the latter is the case, then we need to ask why some objects mattered and others did not.

This is especially evident for architectural features that once had had liturgical significance, such as the piscina (a niche set into the wall on the right of the chancel, in which the vessels used in the mass were washed).[22] They usually display a scalloped indentation and a drainage hole, the sacrarium, which carries the water after use to the sanctified ground outside the church. Adjacent to the piscina and sometimes of an architectural piece with it are the sedilia, the seating used by assistant officiants in the mass (see Figure 1). On the right of the chancel was often an aumbry: an alcove let into the wall, with a wooden door to create a cupboard to store vessels and accoutrements.[23] In my observation they are far less common survivals than piscinae and sedilia, perhaps because the north side of the chancel was a socially prestigious location for post-Reformation gentry monuments. However, their failure to survive was also influenced by changes in theology, and consequently liturgy. When the mass was transformed into a commemorative communion, the vessels used did not need to be treated with the same reverence and kept within the especially sacred space of the sanctuary. Also, communion in both kinds required larger vessels and a flagon to contain the wine. In turn, these required a more storage space than the old aumbries provided, so instead parish chests were used.[24] Today, we may view these and other residual architectural features with largely uncomprehending eyes. But how soon did this incomprehension or indifference begin?

The intercessionary economy

Late-medieval theology and liturgy saw an elaboration of the theory of purgatory. This doctrine derives from the earliest years of the Church's history, not the late 12th century as was once thought,[25] and seems to have become the dominant feature in the 'spiritual economy' from about 1450.

In this economy only the most saintly were thought to find a direct path to heaven. The great majority needed to expiate their sins by

Figure 1 Water colour by Frederick Sandys of the combined piscina and sedilia at North Creake, 1852 (NMS NWHCM: 1951.235.1223.B64). As a result of liturgical changes these architectural features became redundant after the Reformation.

spending time (and suffering) in purgatory. (Today the untutored might take depictions of sufferings in purgatory in Dante or contemporary paintings to represent hell itself.[26]) Related to this was a belief in the community of the living and the dead: that not only might the dead, especially the saintly, intercede on behalf of the living, the living could also intercede to expedite the dead's transfer to heaven. In turn, this gave rise to an ever more elaborate material culture of intercession, which found its primary expression in prayers for the dead. Invocations to such prayers abounded. Numerous provisions for them are to be found in late-medieval wills. Patrons often appear in a prayerful pose in stained glass, such as that of Robert Toppes and his family in St Peter Mancroft (see Figure 2) and the Sheltons at Shelton.

Although this might seem essentially a characteristic of the pre-Reformation church, a surprising number of inscribed invocations survived the Reformation. Perhaps this is largely because of the solid and lasting material forms in which they were embodied. For example, they occur on screens like those still at Cawston and South Walsham, and often constituted an element of monuments. There must have been some compunction about destroying expensively sponsored property or interfering with the 'private' monuments of the dead, not least when members of their families were still living.

We should not underestimate the proprietorialism that people felt towards objects and spaces within ostensibly 'public' churches. This is evident, for example, in the (much later, but referring to just before the Reformation) terminology and assumptions of Roger Martyn (see page 18). Early in her reign, Queen Elizabeth issued a proclamation (1560) that, among other things, prohibited the destruction of personal monuments.[27] It was evidently a response to the unbridled zealotry of some individual reformers, and recognized the affronted proprietorialism of those whose family monuments they threatened. Doctrine was all very well, but property rights and filial piety were not to be ignored. Elizabeth's proclamation must have led to the preservation of many invocatory inscriptions that zealots would otherwise have destroyed.

Sometimes the monuments themselves were elaborate. Good examples are the Terry brass still in St John Maddermarket, and the Browne brass from St Stephen's, now in Norwich Castle Museum.[28] In other instances they are rudimentary. For instance, the invocation *orate pro anima* (pray for the soul of ...) often appears on brasses where there is only text. It is impossible to know what proportion of these has been lost. The early 18th-century Norfolk historian Francis Blomefield more than once records invocatory brasses he found loose in churches, piled up in vestries or thrown into parish chests.[29] Others were being torn up and stolen (by no means always for reasons of dogma) even in his day.[30] Where they have survived often they have been moved around, as with an invocatory brass still in St Stephen's (see Figure 3).

A further aspect of the intercessory economy was the multiplication of those in heaven whom it was believed could intercede for the living. The Holy Kin were expanded to 42, drawing on medieval legends about the descendants of Anne, the mother of Mary, and Jesus's cousinage. This is evidenced in dedications to or representations of St Anne (for example, in the historiated initial (fol. 257) in the Ranworth antiphoner of c.1460–80 in St Helen's, Ranworth) as well as more general art-historical evidence of devotion to the elaborated Holy Family during the 15th century.[31]

A later development along similar lines was the Fourteen Holy Helpers, sometimes

Figure 2 Robert Toppes was one of Norwich's richest merchants during the 15th century and a benefactor. His benefactions included the window in St Peter Mancroft where he appears in a invocatory pose with members of his family. (St Peter Mancroft, great east window, detail, bottom right panel.)

believed to intercede in conjunction with the Virgin. This intercessory grouping (in the persons of the Virgin Mary and Child, Saints Catherine, Barbara and Dorothy) might be depicted on the remains of a part of a velvet chasuble from the early 16th century, including the applied decoration known as an 'orphrey'. It was cut down to a rectangle, possibly as the result of the Reformation.[32] It shows all women, and indeed all resistant virgins. The martyr Dorothea of Caesarea was sometimes considered to be the fifteenth Helper.[33]

The cult of the Virgin

This pursuit of persuasive intercessors was most marked in the various cults of the Virgin.[34] Mariology is a recognizable and pervasive feature of late-medieval English religion.[35] An early example from Norwich is the devotions ordained for the 13th-century hospital of St Giles.[36] The Blackfriars had a chantry chapel for the Virgin in the upper end of the south aisle.[37] The central bosses of the two elliptical vaulting layouts of the Cathedral's Bauchun chapel (replaced during the episcopate of James Goldwell, 1472–99), display the Virgin's assumption and coronation. The narrative on the other bosses derives from the tale of a calumniated empress found in the *Gesta Romanorum*, who benefits from seeking the intercession of the Virgin.[38] Examples of personal devotion to Mary include alderman John Cock and his wife, who asked for prayers in the form of a paternoster and an Ave,[39] and Roger and Elizabeth Rugge, whose brass in St John Maddermarket included an image of the Virgin.[40]

Where the parish church itself had a dedication to Mary, the imagery was to the north of the main altar. Where there was a subsidiary dedication it was in a side chapel to the south, as at Aylsham.[41] The bench ends of South Walsham church show fragments of evidence of devotion to the Virgin: some display lines from the Ave Maria and one poppyhead carries a shield invoking her intercession.[42] In 1505, Thomas Speyne gave lands to fund lights here, one before the rood (which would have included a statue of the Virgin) and one to burn before the image of the Virgin.[43] There is also architectural evidence of the late-medieval enthusiasm for the earlier dedication of the church at South Walsham. The tower and porch are 15th century, and there was a gift for a 'new porch' in 1454.[44] The spandrels of the

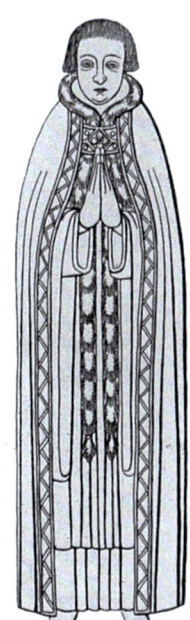

Figure 3 An etching by John Sell Cotman of a brass in St Stephen (1815). It depicts Thomas Capp, vicar there and doctor of the decrees, in his vestments. He was buried on 28 November 1530. The text reflects the prevailing belief in purgatory, invoking prayers for his soul from those who see his brass: 'orate pro anima …'. (NMS NWHCM: 1954.138.Todd7. Mancroft.11.)

porch depict the Virgin and Gabriel – the angel of the Annunciation – with an attenuated symbolic lily. Although defaced, the central niche to the porch still contains a depiction of the Trinity – God the Father, God the Son and the Holy Ghost – with the heavenly Coronation of the Virgin set below them. Other churches in the county also had primary dedications to the Virgin or aspects of her life, and elaborate features reflecting this – examples are Reepham, Tottington and Wiggenhall St Mary.

Perhaps the most spectacular local surviving artefact of the Marian devotion is the Ashwellthorpe triptych altarpiece depicting the 'Seven Sorrows of Mary' of c.1520.[45] In the city the remarkable Annunciation retable now in St Saviour's chapel in the Cathedral (originally from St Michael at Plea) dates from the first half of the 15th century.

In Norwich and elsewhere, churches with a different primary dedication accommodated the devotion to Mary as intercessor by installing chantries, narrative glass or wall painting, and statuary.[46] In Norwich, St Giles had an altar devoted to the Virgin of Pity, supported by a guild of St Mary.[47] A picture of the Virgin of Pity survived in St Michael at Plea into the early 18th century.[48] St Martin at Oak had a similar image.[49] From an institutional viewpoint the major focus of Marian devotion in Norwich was the college of seculars at St Mary in the Fields, on the site of what is now the Assembly House.[50] Before the Reformation it was a focal point for civic and guild processions.[51]

The south aisle of St Michael (or St Miles) Coslany, with its superb external flushwork of interlaced flint and stone, is an architecturally outstanding exemplar.[52] Gregory Clerk, a mercer and alderman who died in 1479, then his son, another Gregory who died in 1516, sponsored its building. At its east end was a chantry chapel for the Virgin endowed by Robert Thorp, also an alderman and an MP for the city – and a sponsor of the aisle as well – who died in 1501. It appears to have been being served by a well-endowed chantry priest before 1505.[53] There was also a chapel of the Virgin at the east end of the south aisle of St John Maddermarket, with a ceiling showing angels holding banderoles invoking the Virgin, and according to Blomefield the Virgin's cipher of a crowned 'M' scattered all over it.[54]

Bells were named and therefore personified: for example one was dedicated to Mary at SS Simon and Jude and another at St Peter Hungate.[55] In contemporary ways of thinking, when they rang the Virgin spoke and interceded for all those who heard them. Bells are relatively likely to survive, while a more exceptional survival is a 15th-century cope from St James, Norwich showing the Virgin in radiance flanked by angels.[56] Since the main dedication is to St James, the cope might have been used at a side (possibly a guild) altar dedicated to the Virgin.[57] Contemporary wills record similar gifts of textiles which have not survived, such as a frontal for the high altar in the Chapel in the Fields in honour of the Virgin, given by the notary William Martyn in 1458.[58]

The female monastery at Carrow, just outside the city walls, held a fair on the vigil of the feast of the Virgin and on the two days following.[59] Again just outside the walls, St Leonard's Priory laid claim to the Virgin's girdle, a symbol of faith in the Virgin's elevation to heaven.[60]

The county had a primary international pilgrimage site at Walsingham with a devotion to the Virgin, which (judging by the recovery rate of pilgrim tokens) had overtaken Canterbury in popularity by 1500. It is likely to have had an impact on parish churches along the routes to the shrine in north Norfolk (especially those with shrines to minor saints),[61] including those in Norwich. St Stephen's had a Lady chapel with an elaborate east window containing the entire history of the Virgin's life, as well as its own locally sanctified 'saint', Richard Caister (see page 17).[62]

In the city in particular the cult of the Virgin may also have been encouraged by women's role in the wave of lay religious enthusiasm, a distinctly urban phenomenon. The humanizing *ecce homo* theme and the devotion of the Lady of Pity must have spoken to the real and painful experiences of many women. Some took their fervent piety further, becoming lay devotees known as 'tertiaries', perhaps associated with a religious order and distinguished by wearing a 'scapular', a garment draped over the shoulders (sometimes shown in devotional paintings).[63] The 15th-century alabaster tablet at St Peter Mancroft depicts five holy women and four virgin martyrs (see Figure 4).[64]

This composite picture of liturgical innovation, in part relating to the Virgin, is supported by the will of John Barker, rector of St Margaret, Westwick, made in 1500. It includes reference to three new orders of service: for the Annunciation, the Transfiguration and the Blessed name of Jesus.[65] In turn, this coincides with evidence from manuscript service books in England that the services for these devotions first became officially recognized around this time[66] – although the material evidence from Norwich suggests that official recognition lagged well behind local practice. So enough survives to demonstrate a lively devotion to the Virgin in the century or so before the Reformation, often specialized on various aspects of her story, reflecting the contemporary preoccupation with intercession, and part of the larger economy of salvation.

The Jesus cult

Closely associated with the cult of the Virgin was the cult of the name of Jesus.[67] As early as 1400 Robert Lomynour, a merchant, required that a high-quality

Figure 4 A 19th century drawing of an alabaster carving in St Peter Mancroft. It depicts the Five Holy Women and Four Virgin Martyrs. (NMS, NWHCM: 1951.235.B34.)

candle burn night and day before the high altar in St Andrew's in honour of Christ's body.[68] The evidence from Norwich wills is that this devotion became popular after 1450.[69] For example, at St Peter Mancroft the altar in the chapel at the east end of the north aisle was dedicated jointly to Jesus and St John the Baptist. A chaplain said daily the Jesus mass, funded by a Jesus guild, founded in 1455.[70] In 1522 the stone memorial to goldsmith John Smart in St Andrew's showed the heart of Jesus.[71] Lady Calthorpe's gift to St Martin at Palace Plain in 1550 included a velvet 'carpet' adorned with roses and lilies and the holy name of Jesus, presumably in the form of the tetragram.[72] This carried the text 'Sicut lilium inter spinas, sic amica mea inter filias' ('As the lily among thorns, so is my love among the daughters': Song of Solomon 2:2).[73] Her quasi-classical monument is still to be seen in the church. Is the plant combining roses and lilies shown in its spandrels intended to be a thorn rose? (There is some dispute amongst biblical scholars over the interpretation of 'rose of Sharon' in the preceding verse. The Vulgate has *lilium*.) Iconographically the tetragram was sometimes surrounded by a crown of thorns, as in the roof of St John Maddermarket.

In addition to the Jesus chapel in the Cathedral where the Jesus mass was said daily, there was a Jesus chapel in the north aisle of St John Maddermarket, with a depiction of the five wounds of Christ.[74] The painted ceiling included Christ's tetragram set within wreaths.[75] The roof boss showing the holy lamb may also have arisen from this devotion,[76] which is explicit elsewhere in the city. The Lamb Inn in Orford Street was so named when the original building was given as a benefaction for the support of the Jesus guild in St Peter Mancroft, and a tenement known in the early 18th century as the Holy Lamb was previously called Jesus Inn.[77]

The Erpingham Gate, one of the main entrances to the Cathedral Close, was built around 1428. Its statuary was a medley of intercessory figures, and more specifically it carried other conventional symbolism for Jesus: not the tetragram IHS, but (above the arch) Christological heraldry, a format perhaps chosen to fit in with its secular dynastic heraldry.[78] The five wounds of Christ (a common and specific Christological devotion) were summarized by a heart set between two hands with two feet at the base (signifying four wounds by nails to hands and feet and the spear to the heart).[79] Interestingly, the same type of 'wound' symbolism appears on the surviving Erpingham chasuble, where four angels hold vessels to collect the blood of Christ from his wounds.[80] Perhaps the gate's sponsor, Sir Thomas Erpingham, personally chose this symbolism, often associated with men at arms. Another soldier, John Wodehouse, who died in 1430, founded a chantry in the undercroft of the Carnary – itself an ossuary – to the left of this gate, and itself dedicated to the Holy Trinity (like the Cathedral) and to the five wounds of Christ.[81] Was there the potential for this to develop into a devotional cluster? Norfolk produced many military entrepreneurs in the 14th and 15th centuries.[82]

The implications of cults

The development of cults focused on aspects of the Virgin and of Christ illuminates a number of issues. First, they demonstrate the vibrancy and the continuing evolving character of late-medieval religion. Second, it is evident that they were driven by the preoccupation with intercession. For the name of Jesus there was a basis in John 16:23, 'Verily, verily, I say unto you, Whatsoever ye shall ask the Father in my name he will give it you.' In Matthew 1:21 giving the name 'Jesus' is presented as being both divinely inspired and intimately related to the forgiveness of sins (see also Paul in Romans 10:13).

Third, the tetragram of Christ's name was used in a way that suggests it was perhaps seen as totemic.[83] It was commonly believed that people could obtain apotropaic protection or talismanic benefit by wearing objects bearing religious symbols or emblems. An example is a surviving medieval copper alloy ring badge which originally enclosed a fleur-de-lys, the emblem of the Virgin Mary.[84] To its wearer it was more than a symbol: it was in itself a potent object open to invocation. These personal 'decorative' objects also exemplified the intercessory culture, and suggest how frequently those who wore or carried them thought of intercession.

Fourth, the proliferation of ever-more-specialized devotional cults indicates the opportunities in late-medieval Christianity for individuals to select and personalize their own particular devotion. Emphasis on the maternal role of Mary and on the human rather than the divine and lordly dimension of Jesus more readily brought comfort to those seeking solace, especially women. Similarly, the wounds of Christ had a special relevance for military entrepreneurs. Individuals became attached to locations within a church, and to devotional objects in those spaces, which provided foci for these personalized devotions. In effect, this personalized the space within the church as a whole. The proliferation of secondary altars, chantry chapels, statuary and so on must have encouraged proprietorialism, even by those who had not paid for them. Many must have felt the depredations inflicted by the Reformation as a highly personal loss.[85] Furthermore research in recent decades has demonstrated how devotional practices devolved from the sophisticated thinking of the theologians and gained a more demotic overlay.

Personalization, totemism and augmentation

In summary, we can perhaps identify three main aspects to this demotic, more colloquial expression of religious sentiment: personalization, totemism and augmentation. Personalization arose not least because individuals and groups such as guilds were encouraged by the economy of salvation to invest in objects for use in the rituals of the liturgy and to adorn their church. For example, guilds generally had a bier cloth to cover the coffin during obsequies for dead members.[86] In wills there are innumerable provisions for 'lights': candles to be placed in a specific part of the church on a designated day such as an individual's name day, which was almost always also a saint's day.

This implies two things. First, it shows the articulation of and ongoing provision for a distinctive personal devotion. For example, in 1507, Julian Stedman of Litcham actually left his bee hives to the church in order to provide the wax for the candles that he wanted to burn before selected images, for 'as long as it pleasyth god to kepe the sey benne [bees]'.[87] Second, the implication is that family and friends would gather in that place in the church on memorial days to recall the departed. In itself this was one of the liturgical mechanisms that bound together the living with the dead within the confines of the parish church. In Norwich the provision for temporary chantries and annuals of masses reached its peak between 1490 and 1517.[88]

Items for use in services such as altar frontals or liturgical vessels might carry the name of wealthy donors and requests for prayers for their souls. An example is two silver dishes given by Sir Thomas Kerdiston in 1448 to the Augustinian canons.[89] Some wills make it clear that an individual had a special devotion to a favourite saint or intercessor which they wanted to see continued after death, for example by leaving highly personal items such as rosary

Figure 5 An officiant administers the mass accompanied by two acolytes and two servers who hold a houseling cloth for catching any crumbs from the wafer. A detail from a Flemish Book of Hours of the early 16th century. (Oxford, Bodleian Library, MS Douce 112, fol.21r, detail.)

beads to adorn a particular statue. Thus, in 1509 Beatrix Krikemer, buried in St Stephen's, bequeathed 'to our Lady ... my best beads to hang about her neck on good days'.[90] During life personalization through objects extended to wearing items reflecting specific personal devotions. For example, metal (usually copper or copper alloy) belt ends to girdles were intended to replicate the girdle that the Virgin had dropped from heaven in order to persuade St Thomas of her Assumption. Such girdles were also thought to ease childbirth.[91]

The evident devotion to specific objects, especially statuary, indicates that many ordinary parishioners saw efficacious transformative magic as residing in the object rather than in what it represented. The vociferousness with which reformers condemned this practice suggests that this was well recognized at the time. Anthropologists describe this as 'totemism'. Higher theology makes a clear distinction between the object and what it represents, but totemistic practices are understandable in the context of other teachings. In transubstantiation, the wafer and the wine were (and by some still are) believed to turn into the very body and blood of Christ.

More generally there was a commonplace assumption in this era that components of the material world contained magical and manipulable properties. At times individuals attempted to 'capture' the magic claimed by the Church their own purposes. As a manuscript illustration illustrates, great care was taken to ensure that no crumbs from the communion wafer were dropped and later purloined.[92] (See Figure 5.) For the same reason communicants were given a mixture of water and wine – something of no theological significance – to ensure that they swallowed the wafer and did not go off with it to use in their own magic. Finally, the vessels that had held the body and blood of Christ themselves contained strong magic by their association, and perhaps some people believed the vessels achieved the transubstantiation. For this reason as much as any fear of theft for monetary value, they were kept locked in the aumbry within the sacrosanct space of the sanctuary, and needed to be washed in the piscina (see Figure 1).

For the same reasons fonts had to be kept secure. They contained the chrism, a mixture of olive oil and balm, which was added to water that had been blessed. As with much else in the medieval church, something that had a practical liturgical purpose – the font cover – became the occasion for decorative elaboration reflecting the importance of transformative properties. Some medieval font coverings in Norfolk are truly magnificent, as at Elsing (which retains some original colouring), Salle (where the pulley necessary to raise it survives on an extended arm from the balcony), Trunch (where the canopy of 1500 outshines the modest font that it covers and is one of the best in the country), and in Norwich at St Peter Mancroft (after 1463; only the top section is Victorian restoration).

Finally, augmentation occurred when a wider array of popular beliefs and practices became entwined with properly sanctioned theological beliefs and liturgical practices. This might involve taking sanctified objects out of the church (such as those purloined communion wafers), or carrying into the church markers of popular magical beliefs: the graffiti now increasingly being identified in churches provide good examples.[93] As at Swannington, the concentration of these types of graffiti may indicate the location of now-lost side altars, guild chapels or devotional imagery.[94]

Reformation and change

But then came the theological revolution. The belief in purgatory was rejected, and with it went the complex culture of intercession and its material expressions. The rejection of purgatory is stated clearly in one of the foundation documents of the new Church in England: 'The Romish doctrine concerning Purgatory, Pardons, worshipping and adoration as well of Images as of Relics, and also Invocation of Saints, is a fond thing vainly invented, and grounded upon no warranty of Scripture; but rather repugnant to the word of God.'[95] In England there had been some flirtation with Lutheran beliefs in the 1530s and 1540s, but in the end it was not Luther but Calvin's reformed theology that for three or four generations became the official doctrine of the new Tudor dynastic Church.[96] In spite of all the disputes over vestments and forms of church government that riddled the Elizabethan church, there was an underlying agreement on theology between the episcopacy and those who wanted further reform of other aspects of the Church. A fundamental of Calvin's severely logical theology of salvation was the notion of double predestination. This asserted that as God was omniscient and existed beyond time, He had ordained who was saved and who was damned. No amount of good works or prayer could purchase salvation. Rather, people needed to examine themselves for signs of salvation. Contrary to what is often assumed, predestination was not central to Calvin's thought. However, it took on new meaning in the theology of Theodore Beza, Calvin's successor in Geneva, and Beza was immensely influential in Elizabethan and early Stuart England.[97] There are three volumes by him in the Norwich Old Library, set up in 1608 for the use of preachers in the civic Green Yard adjacent to St Andrew's Hall.[98]

Among other things Beza promulgated the notion of 'election'. This involved the equation of reformed congregations with the people of Israel as the chosen ones. The philo-hebraism that it fostered is to be read in the sermons of the period. This is of especial significance in our local context. In the countryside enthused local gentry such as Nathaniel Bacon on the north Norfolk coast used their secular authority as magistrates to foster 'godliness' and to suppress reprobates in the communities they oversaw.[99] A large city such as Norwich afforded Biblical parallels: as preachers variously suggested, was it to be a New Jerusalem, a city set upon a hill, a beacon to others? Or were the problems created by its teeming population demonstrative of an irredeemable latter-day Sodom or Gomorrah? For a number of generations in Norwich there was a close alliance between magistracy and ministry, a faction among its ruling elite and local pastors, through which they tried to realize the former and expunge the latter model. So Dante's earlier theology of purgatory and eventual redemption was replaced by Calvin's implacable god, and given a local habitation. In turn this fundamental theological revolution found expression in a transformation in the material culture of parish churches.

The sounds of sanctity across the city

A number of architectural components remind us that liturgical practice was not limited to the confines of the church: it spread out across the surrounding countryside and into the city's streets. I am not sure to what extent an angelus bell – rung at 6 am, noon and 6 pm as a call for prayer to those about their daily tasks – was used in the pre-Reformation churches of Norwich.[100] The custom originated in monastic practice in the 11th century, then was taken up by the friars, initially the Franciscans, so at the least it would have been heard from the churches of the religious orders.[101]

In addition the sanctus bell was rung at two points during the mass, including the moment when the elevated host was believed to be transformed into the body of Christ. Usually this was a small bell in an external 'turret' at the east end of the nave. A number survive around the county, although others are Victorian reinstallations.[102] At Melton Constable there is still a seat for the person responsible for sounding the bell.[103] Since we know a huge number of masses were funded to be said in the city, the sounds of these bells must have been almost continual. This brings home the point that there was no clear division between obviously sacred places such as parish churches and – in our anachronistic terms – wholly 'secular' parts of the urban space. The angelus bell was also significant for linking the diurnal rhythm with a longer temporal cycle reflecting the lives of Christ and Mary that occupied distinct parts of the liturgical year. The sanctus bell reminded everyone that for their salvation the body of Christ was being sacrificed somewhere at that moment. Other evidence comes from the fortuitous survival of private and domestic devotional objects such as manuscript books. So we can think of the city as being pervaded by the sounds of the sacred, a numinous place with Christ brought within it by the daily liturgical round.

Processions

St Gregory's, St Peter Mancroft and St John Maddermarket still have under-arches at the east end, which remind us that liturgy was not confined to inside the church, but that periodic and peripatetic aspergement (the sprinkling of holy water) in order to sanctify spaces and places called for processions.[104] These were ordered according to the arrangements set out in the practical service books that figured largely in the wills of the secular (parochial) clergy in Norwich.[105] The contemporary institutional organization of the urban world also encouraged processions, as a means of representing solidarities such as guilds and the over-arching municipal authority. Streets, lanes and open spaces provided a stage. Various civic ordinances in Norwich, such as those of 1449 and 1543, specified how the crafts were to fulfil their obligations, including participating in an annual sequence of processions.

Earlier, these processions also provided the genesis of the peripatetic Whitsun performances which dramatized aspects of the Christian story. The development of the feast of Corpus Christi resulted in a procession specifically of the secular clergy (observed by the laity). It went along Lady Lane (now lost, but where the Forum is today) to the Chapel in the Fields.[106] Individual parish churches and other religious institutions in the City also set up irregular processions: for instance, of guild members to funerals. In 1425 Bishop Wakerying gave a sense of what this meant, in admonishing that 'I want the vigils of the dead to be performed in the ordinary way immediately after my death, without elaborate ceremonies and processions, which solace the living, according to the blessed Augustine, rather than help the dead.'[107] Finally, wills of the early 16th century[108] mention a group of minor pilgrimage sites, all within 20 miles of Norwich and three – Bawburgh, Cringleford and Horstead – within 7 miles. These were probably convenient destinations for processions from the City on feast days such as that of St Walstan at Bawburgh on 30 May.

Outdoor religious imagery

These outdoor religious activities were also encouraged by devotional images in the form of statuary outside churches and crosses in churchyards, in the city's streets and on its boundaries. The crosses seem to have been locations for preaching. After the Reformation the cross in the Cathedral Close expanded into a preaching or 'green yard'.[109]

There was an image of the Virgin 'in the alley in the churchyard' at SS Simon and Jude and an image of the Trinity in a niche in the west side of the tower of St Giles.[110] Blomefield remarked laconically of the Virgin in the oak in the churchyard of St Martin at Oak that 'What particular virtue, this good lady had, I do not know, but certain it is, she was much visited by the populace, who left many gifts in their wills, to dress, paint, and repair her.'[111]

Some open-air crosses stood in churchyards, as in the case of Martin's cross in the south part of the churchyard at St Martin in the Bailey, St Stephen's and St Giles.[112] The cross at St Crowche's, renewed in 1479, was in the north of the churchyard, as was the one at St Michael at Plea.[113] In 1533 it was requested that the cross in the churchyard of St George's Colegate be moved to the top of a tomb.[114]

In Norwich market a covered cross was erected in 1453 for the sale of grain.[115] The main, octagonal market cross combined commerce with religion: there were four shops in it but also a chapel. It had prominent crosses on its corners, and was served more or less daily by the chaplain to the Guildhall.[116] The toponym 'Charing Cross' in the parish of St John Maddermarket is a corruption of 'Sherer's cross', a stone structure.[117] The 'stump cross' at the junction of Magdalen Street and St Botolph's Street survived being demolished in 1644 and replaced in 1673 and is still remembered today.[118] Another public cross stood at the junction of what is now Cross Street and Calvert Street.[119]

These crosses served religious purposes but also often marked boundaries, imparting to them a condition of liminality, or 'betweenness'. They were potent objects that opened the gates between this world and the next, so they became antennae for the broadcast of intercessory requests. When in 1502 Thomas Batchcroft paid for the building of Earlham bridge across the Yare, a few miles west of the city, he specified that a stone cross be erected adjacent to it, inscribed with a request for prayers for him and members of his family.[120] Of course the pinch-point of the bridge was a good place to catch prospective earthly supplicants.

For convenience many of the numerous religious houses across Norfolk maintained premises in the city. In 1317 the prior and monks of Bromholm purchased a house in the parish of All Saints Timber Hill. In the medieval and early-modern city large and colourful signs identified major properties which sometimes gave their name to the street, as with Red Lion Street and Rampant Horse Street. The brothers of Bromholm were custodians of a fragment of the Holy Cross, and their Norwich house, called 'the Holy Cross of Bromholm', probably displayed its image.[121]

Crosses indicated the city's external and internal boundaries, since numerous enclaves – mainly ecclesiastical – were excluded from its jurisdiction. At one point the boundary between the City and the liberty of the Close was marked by a stone cross surmounted by a statue of St Michael.[122] Another cross, at Harford bridges, marked the boundary between the county and the city. Judging by a benefaction in 1452 it carried a representation of Christ on the cross.[123] Today signs on approach roads describe Norwich as 'A Fine City'; in the medieval period it announced itself as a truly Christian city.

Certain services were held in the open each year, such as Palm Sunday, at locations known as 'palm crosses': in the west of St Stephen's churchyard, in the large churchyard of St Augustine's, and in stone at St Peter Mancroft, which judging by contemporary allusions became a familiar point of reference.[124] When this moveable feast fell early, willow with its catkins was substituted for palm, as we know from other parts of the country: this may account for the name of Willow Lane near St Giles.[125] Processions on festival of the cross or holy rood day (Exaltatio Sancte Crucis, 14 September) often headed for these crosses.[126] The church of the Invention of the Holy Cross (or St Crowche's) closed at the Reformation but was previously a place of pilgrimage. Those who visited it earned an indulgence of 300 days remission from purgatory.[127]

Large and impressive architectural endowments such as Sir Thomas Erpingham's could help to shape devotional enthusiasms, including those related to the cross. Sir Thomas funded a monk to say mass daily at an altar in the cathedral that was dedicated to the Holy Cross.[128] He was also largely responsible for funding the building of the Blackfriars, where his arms are displayed externally on the nave, and an altar at the east end of the nave was dedicated to the Holy Cross and supported by a guild.[129] For a time the cross marking the grave of Bishop John of Oxford in the Cathedral was a pilgrimage destination and staging point in processions.[130]

Some evidence suggests there were increasing numbers of processions in late-medieval Norwich, not only around churches but through the city and beyond. The development of the Easter sepulchre for tombs – perhaps more evident in the county than in the city – hints at the social appropriation of this proximity to salvation. It was also the origin in space and the annual cycle (in the especially complex Easter liturgy) of one strand of medieval drama, whose material practicalities informed the less ephemeral material culture of the stonemason and the glazier, crafts that flourished in late-medieval Norwich. In these ways it was becoming a 'performative city'.

Banner stave cupboards in churches stored the staves, and possibly banners, carried in processions, and perhaps also processional crosses. As early as 1368, St Peter Mancroft had four banners in its inventory.[131] We know of such crosses in Norwich at St Martin at Oak, All Saints, possibly St Mary the Less, St Peter Mancroft and Carrow Priory, and there were probably more.[132]

The ornate west doors that grace many Norwich and Norfolk churches, often remade in the 15th century in association with towers, are today almost always locked and frequently neglected, but they played an important role in processions.[133] 'First-floor' ringing chambers (as at St Peter Mancroft and Cawston) did not impede processions and did provide musical accompaniment. The decoration of the door surrounds, especially in the spandrels, and the statuary that once occupied adjacent niches (as at St Michael Coslany) may well have indicated what particular processions passed under these entrance, obtaining blessings from the censing angels in the spandrels (as at St Michael at Plea)[134] or the titular saint. The processions gave lively meaning to statuary and carving which now might appear as mere incidental decoration.

Palm Sunday and Easter Week made substantial use of processions within the churchyard.[135] In some forms of service this involved the doors initially being closed, with a Latin hymn sung by a small number of voices within the church echoed back by those outside the church before the doors were opened and all entered. Palm Sunday was the preliminary to the even more dramatic events the following weekend which took place in the sanctuary and which focused on the Easter sepulchre.

Dress

The performance of the liturgy and participation in processions required specialized dress for some participants. In the 15th century England was famous for embroidered vestments, or *opus Anglicanum*. The colour, feel, drape and decoration of textiles was an important part of the material culture. Only a few garments survive, often, as with the Bircham cope of c.1480, because they were converted to other uses (here, an altar frontal) (Figure 6).[136] There are surviving examples in diocesan museums in Italy and in the V&A.[137] 'In action', elaborate vestments combined with the development of the Corpus Christi festivity helped to mark out the priest as the ordained intercessor for his congregation.[138]

Screens

In Norfolk, as in Devon, many rood screens survive at least in part (perhaps around a hundred). Providing a fundamental division between the chancel and the nave, under the rood itself – Christ on the cross – they imply the conjointness of the living and the dead; of the progression through each individual church that modelled the larger body of the entire Church: from the Church Militant in the nave to the Church Triumphant in the chancel.[139]

Parclose screens surrounded chantries, and multiplied in this period. Few survived the Reformation, but there are examples at Walpole St Peter, the Spring chantry at Lavenham, and the Harling chapel at East Harling.[140] Panels possibly from the chapel of St Mary in St John Maddermarket are now in the V&A.[141] One was funded by Ralph Skeet for the chapel of St Barbara at the upper end of the north aisle in the Blackfriars.[142] Partial documentation gives us some inkling of the increasingly crowded spaces of the late-

Figure 6 The Bircham cope. Detail of an orphrey from an original cope later reused to form a border to an altar frontal. It shows a demi-angel with three sets of wings. (NMS NWHCM: 1939.75.)

medieval church.[143] To the screens must be added separate and specialized side and nave altars, candles and statuary.

In summary, judicious collation of documentary references, surviving artefacts and remaining architectural components lets us reconstitute much of late-medieval liturgical practice 'on the ground' and infer something of the experience of participants and observers.

The Reformation

The changes when they came were harsh and immediate. One of the most treasured possessions of St Edmund's was a crystal reliquary reputed to contain a portion of the shirt of the eponymous local saint, a minor object of pilgrimage.[144] Within a generation it was gone. It was supplanted by radical preacher, Henry Bird, a man of the word, the book and the pulpit (see Figure 7).[145] Under the promptings of reformers such as Hugh Latimer, regular preaching became the watchword. This vision is epitomized by the lower left-hand side of the frontispiece to the *Greate Bible* of 1539. The admonitory preacher is surrounded by an attentive audience. Above him the word descends from God to the king, then via preaching to his people.[146] Similar scenes appear in the Bishops' Bible of 1569 and John Foxe's *Actes and Monumentes* of 1563, the new Protestant martyrology. St Andrew's still has the rabid assertions inscribed on the boards now at the west end of the nave celebrating an escape from idolatry and the coming of the new light.[147]

In Binham, north Norfolk, the transition from image to word is shown in a rood screen overwritten with texts from Tyndale's translation of the Bible. Today, in places the overpainting has worn away and the heads of saints and angels peek through the gothic letters (Figure 8). From the 1560s a revolution in the education of the clergy ensured that an increasing number were qualified to preach and to fill the pulpits. Certainly, this was the case in the diocese of Norwich.[148]

When we consider what replaced the rich texture of life experience imparted by the material culture of late medieval religious practice, we encounter an irony and a paradox.

The medieval material record may be depleted, but more survives today than for the period immediately following. There is very little remaining evidence for the material culture and liturgical practice in parish churches between roughly the 1540s and the 1620s. If he was to return today Henry Bird would be shocked by the appearance of Anglican churches, and especially in Norwich, which in the course of the 19th and 20th centuries appear to have been taken over by high-church Anglicans.

One reason for this paucity of evidence is that those early generations of reformers defined themselves against many of the forms of materiality of the late-medieval church. For them salvation lay in the word, not the object. They obliterated much within parish churches but left little evidence of their – at the time – vociferous presence.

It is not that they ignored objects; rather, for them religious objects took on a heightened significance. But usually they were markers of all they abhorred. The vessels and accoutrements of the mass were replaced by the new types of vessel, including cups and flagons, required by communion in both kinds. In turn, this arose from a new theological interpretation of the eucharist as a re-enactment of the last supper, not the sacrificial suffering in the field of Golgotha. Mary Fewster has demonstrated how providing them kept Norwich goldsmiths busy for upwards of 20 years.[149] Much surviving silverwork is in the Cathedral treasuries in Norwich and Bury St Edmunds (see Figure 9).

This aversion elevated the object to totemic status while at the same time denying all objects – most especially the wine and the wafer – transformative potency. In 1565, in a sermon, one Cambridge academic attacked the use of unleavened bread in the eucharist, calling it 'starch and paste'.[150] In the 1560s 'Vestiarian controversy' forward protestants objected to the use of ecclesiastical vestments that for them carried unwelcome associations with catholicism, and implied the intercessory role of the priest.[151] At Cambridge in the 1570s there was a scandal when Thomas Legge, president of Gonville & Caius College, was found to have stashed away 'the trumpery of popery' in the hope of its future reinstatement. This phrase is implied visually in woodcuts depicting objects of catholic religious practice being crushed under the heel of a triumphant protestant 'Faith' (Figure 10). Thirty years later in north Norfolk when the JP Nathaniel

Figure 7 The changing face of the clergy: portrait of Henry Bird, 'preacher' at St Edmunds, Norwich, aged 60 in 1583 (NMS NWHCM: 1935.130). Currently on display in Strangers' Hall, Norwich.

Figure 8 The image replaced by the word: a section of the former rood screen at Binham, north Norfolk. The pre-Reformation painting of saints was overwritten with text from Tyndale's Bible. Over time the saints have begun to reappear.

Bacon carried out a dawn raid on the home of a recusant neighbour, Francis Woodhouse, he reported discovery of 'the toyes of popery'.[152]

For evidence of parochial life under the new protestant pastors we have look at the sermons they once delivered, an unknown proportion of which have been preserved. Nicholas Bownd, incumbent at St Andrew's, claimed his predecessor delivered 'many hundred sermons, or rather certain thousands' during his 20 years in Norfolk, preaching every day and sometimes twice on Sundays. But today we have only *Three Godly and Fruitfull Sermons* through which to view messianic John More, the 'Apostle of Norwich'.[153]

In at least some churches, text replaced imagery in the form of detached panels and scrolls and cartouches painted on walls. Many boards carrying in English the Lord's Prayer, the Ten Commandments and the Creed survive. The churchwardens of St Mary Coslany paid five marks 'to the paynter for wryting upon the wall in the church necessary scryptures'. Similar texts were put up at Shipdham and Swaffham during Edward's reign, only to be painted over under Mary. Texts were also introduced at St Andrew's.[154] A 19th-century watercolour shows a scroll discovered in 1850 on the south wall of St John and Holy Sepulchre.[155] Godparents

Figure 9 Much of the new communion plate required as a result of theological and liturgical changes at the Reformation was produced by Norwich's goldsmiths. This is a typical Norwich-made communion cup, from Colby, dated 1568. (NMS, NWHCM: L1996.T354 D.)

were required to ensure that their godchildren learned, in English, the Prayer, Commandments and Creed, so these painted texts gave the church building itself a quasi-paternal or patronal role. This experience echoed the patron–client relations that permeated contemporary society, or even suggested its inevitability and desirability.[156]

Illustration was not abandoned entirely, but the subject matter changed as a result of changes in theology. At West Walton, in the arcade spandrels, the emblems of the Twelve Tribes of Israel (said to have been overpainted in the 18th century) reflect Beza's influence.[157] Among contemporary modes of thought was the long-established practice of typology, proposing that events in the Old Testament foretold those in the New Testament (as the 12 disciples echo the 12 tribes of Israel). Some saw the messianic preachers of the day as the new apostles.

Text and Old Testament imagery were combined on a 17th-century panel displaying the Commandments supported by Moses and Aaron.[158] Biblical admonitions also appear on the 'oblongel' trenchers that may have been used in the great Guild Feast, the highpoint of civic life in post-reformation Norwich. One depicts the Biblical parable of the rich man and Lazarus (Luke 16: 19–31).[159]

At Walsoken three-dimensional representations of two rulers and judges of Israel face one another down the nave. Above the tower arch is a naive wooden sculpture (see Figure 11), with painted figures that make clear it is meant to show the Judgement of Solomon. The figure is apparently derived from a woodcut of Henry VIII, the biblically sanctioned king sitting in majesty. The English identity is reinforced by the angel floating above the king-figure bearing the coat of arms of England. Over the chancel arch, David plays his harp surmounted by another angel bearing the arms of England.

Reformers during Edward's reign required communion to be taken at an ordinary table set in the body of the church.[160] Current Anglican liturgical practice preserves nothing of this arrangement, but we see it in contemporary prints (see Figure 12). St Andrew's paid 5s. for their new table.[161] Some tables survive, not always with their significance understood. The oval table standing idly in the aisle at Southwold was installed by the billeted Presbyterian Scots in the 1650s. The note attached to a substantial long table now in the narthex of Walpole St Peter suggests it came from a local manor house, but it would not have been inappropriate as a communion table set longitudinally in the chancel.[162] The Edwardian communion table at North Walsham is now (uncomprehendingly) used as an altar in a side chapel.

The protagonists of the 'Beauties of Holiness' during their ascendancy in the 1620s and 1630s also contributed to the lack of surviving material culture from the immediate post-Reformation years. They believed true devotion required seemliness, reverence, solemnity and ceremony.[163] The material expression of this set of beliefs was not the post-Reformation ecclesiastical art of England: it was a reaction against the modest embellishment of parish churches and the spartan practice of the liturgy of the Prayer Book of 1563, printed in around 290 editions between 1549 and 1642.[164] By the 1620s this had become the new 'normal'.

In material terms the beautification of holiness required the reinstallation of altars at the east end, a raised step in the chancel, the railing-in of the altar and the readoption of seemly and decorative font covers. An excellent example is Walpole St Peter's stepped altar with original Laudian railings. Wiggenhall St Mary the Virgin has a delightful painted font cover surmounted by a pelican-in-piety dated 1625 (Figure 13). The pelican was an old symbol of Christ's sacrifice of his blood.[165]

Figure 10 (left) A personification of 'Faith' tramples on objects used in catholic forms of worship. Elsewhere they are referred to as the 'toyes', 'trumpery' or 'pilfery' of popery. This illustrates that theological differences articulated through liturgy ultimately were expressed in material terms. Detail from [John Day], *A booke of Christian prayers, collected out of the auncie[n]t writers, and best learned in our tyme, worthy to be read with an earnest mynde of all Christians, in these daungerous and troublesome dayes*, ... (London, 1581) fol.62. STC2 6430. In its various editions this was generally known as 'Queene Elizabeth's prayer book' from the depiction of the queen in the frontispiece and the claim to having been printed with royal approval. Day and his brother were religious radicals.

Figure 11 (right) Philo-hebraism: Walsoken, west Norfolk, west end tower arch, the Judgement of Solomon.

Figure 12 (right) Depiction of 'The Lord's Supper' from *Eniautos, or, A course of catechising being the marrow of all orthodox and practical expositions upon the church-catechism* (London, 1674) opposite p. 276. Communicants are gathered around a 'holy table' set longitudinally.

Figure 13 (below) 'Laudian' font cover, painted wood inscribed 'M.F.P.H 1.6.2.5'; surmounted by a 'pelican in piety' (formerly in the church of Wiggenhall St Mary the Virgin).

LORDS SUPPER

To win the war in the diocese the Laudians needed to win the battle in Norwich's parish churches. The new decorous font cover of 1637 still at St Andrew's was an affront to this most radical of Norwich congregations. Outraged prayer-book Anglicans and more radical protestants laid these innovations at the door of Bishop Wren and Archbishop Laud in the Long Parliament of the 1640s.[166]

Another reason for the paucity of material evidence concerns the attenuation of social distance during the 18th century and a new privatization of space in the church. This resulted in the horror that is the box pew. Fourth and finally, the combination of 19th-century ecclesiology and the High Church movement resulted in a thoroughgoing campaign to rehistoricize the parish church. This was not simply driven by aesthetic concerns, but represented an attempt to return to what was – is? – perceived to be the authenticity of medieval catholic theology as expressed in the liturgy and its material setting.

Conclusion

There was a time when historians interpreted the reformation in terms of abstruse disputes about theology or – especially in England – in terms of the exigencies of high politics and acts of state. In the last 20 years there has been a refreshing concern with the changing experiences of the religion of ordinary people. Also, an increasing number of local studies have detailed the mechanics of change. However, what has been attempted here is a return to consideration of theology and liturgy but in a new way that tries to marry this up with the evidence provided by material culture, both that which survives and that which we can know about by other means. From this we may infer somewhat about the experience of religion and religious change. As I have suggested, change and innovation were as much a feature of pre- as of post-Reformation Norwich.

The translation of theology into liturgy results in the specific symbolic organization of space and the precise imputation of meaning to objects used in worship; the demeanour required of those who handle them; and the ritual uses to which space and objects in the church are put. In this way, for most people, the Reformation was experienced through the changing appearance of spaces – usually the space of their parish church – the objects they saw before them and the ways in which those objects were deployed. In addition, as I have tried to outline here, in a city such as Norwich the experience of the liturgy was not confined to the parish church but was part of an encompassing urban spiritual topography. In effect, the reformation was a revolution in the experience of material life, and nowhere more so than in the teeming crucible that was Norwich with its plenitude of parish churches and religious practices.

Dr Victor Morgan *(now semi-retired) has been senior lecturer in early modern history at UEA, director of the Centre of East Anglian Studies, and a tutor in higher education practice in the Centre for Staff Development. He has published in the areas of the history of the universities, the history of cartography and perceptions of space, patronage and clientage, Tudor and Stuart portraiture, emblems, great houses, ritual and ceremony, local government and society. He is currently editing, with others, Volume VI of* The Papers of Nathaniel Bacon of Stiffkey, *a study of civic ritual in Norwich, and a general history of the City, c.1450–1750.*

Notes

The following abbreviations are used in these notes:
NMS   Norfolk Museums Service
Blomefield   F. Blomefield and C. Parkin, *A Essay towards a Topographical History of Norfolk*, 11 vols. Norwich, 1805–11.

1   This paper adds to the documentary evidence provided in my original talk.
2   V. Morgan, 'Presidential address: My life among things: material objects and the immaterial world', *The Annual* (Bulletin of the Norfolk Archaeological and Historical Research Group), 10 (2001), pp. 61–72.
3   For comparative studies see e.g. Patrick Collinson and John Craig (eds), *The Reformation in English Towns, 1500–1640* (Basingstoke, 1998). My approach is rather different from that in this volume.
4   The debate over the 'great rebuilding' of vernacular houses in the early-modern period has demonstrated that the chronology cannot simply be read from surviving material evidence

(see W. G. Hoskins, 'The rebuilding of rural England, 1570–1640', *Past and Present*, 4 (1953), pp. 44–59; R. Machin, 'The great rebuilding: a reassessment', *Past and Present,* 77 (1977), pp. 33–56; C. R. J. Currie, 'Time and chance: modelling the attrition of old houses', *Vernacular Architecture*, 19 (1988), pp.1–9.

5   C. H. Lawrence, *Medieval Monasticism: Forms of Religious Life in Western Europe in the Middle Ages* (2nd edn; London and New York, 1989), p. 231.

6   V. Morgan, 'Reprise and prospect: the 'great house' in Norfolk, circa 1450–1750', *Journal of the Norfolk Historic Buildings Group*, 1 (2002–3) pp. 35–52.

7   For a masterly continent-wide summary see N. Yates, *Liturgical Space: Christian Worship and Church Buildings in Western Europe, 1500–2000* (Aldershot, 2008).

8   See the lozenge frieze above the west doorway with a datestone of 1550.

9   D. Summers, 'Grand community projects: Norfolk church towers of the late middle ages', *Journal of the Norfolk Historic Buildings Group*, 3 (2007) pp. 109–17.

10 Tanner, *Church in Norwich*, pp. 35–7.

11 Norfolk Museums Service (NMS), KILLM: 1978.196.175.

12 The de la Poles, earls of Suffolk, were long-time lords of the main manor in Cawston and one married a Wingfield heiress (F. Blomefield and C. Parkin, *An Essay Towards a Topographical History of Norfolk*, 11 vols, Norwich, 1805–11, vi, pp. 257–8, 265).

13 Blomefield, viii, p. 274.

14 Blomefield, viii, pp. 276; iv, p. 216.

15 See V. Morgan, 'Visit to East Barsham Manor House', *Aylsham Local History Society Journal*, 9 (2011), pp. 66–73.

16 NMS, NWHCM: L1971.18. It later became part of an altar frontal. Westgate served as an alderman between 1524 and 1526 and probably died in the latter year. He had been a sheriff in 1520 and chamberlain 1510–11 (T. Hawes (comp.), *An Index to Norwich City Officers 1453–1835*, Norfolk Record Society 52, 1989, p.163).

17 C. Paine and D. Dymond, *The Spoil of Melford Church: The Reformation in a Suffolk Parish* (1989).

18 See P. Cattermole and S. Cotton, 'Medieval parish church building in Norfolk', *Norfolk Archaeology*, 38 (1983), pp. 35–79. The current Leverhulme-funded project on Norwich churches is likely to add substantially to our understanding of this topic.

19 Tanner, *The Church in Norwich*, p. 4. For a recent summary of Tanner's wider findings for the City see his *The Church in the Later Middle Ages* (London and New York, 2008), pp. 56–69.

20 Lollardy was a presence in East Anglia, and Henry Despencer, bishop of Norwich (1370–1406) was one of its implacable opponents. It was also a theological dispute resolved into material objects. Thus it has been argued that the seven-sacrament fonts to be found in East Anglia are an assertion of orthodoxy against Lollard heterodoxy (see A. E. Nichols, *Seeable Signs: The Iconography of the Seven Sacraments, 1350–1544*, Woodbridge, 1994). The Lollards' Pit in Thorpe is the site of the execution of those found guilty of Lollardy. The degree of continuity between Lollardy and early protestantism is a matter of debate. Possibly it primarily reflects 16th-century reformers' desire for historical precedent and justification.

21 Stephen Greenblatt, *Hamlet in Purgatory* (Princeton, N.J., 2013).

22 19th-century antiquarian drawings often record details: for example the piscina in St Peter Southgate, incorrectly catalogued as a 'stoop' (NMS, NWHCM: 1954.138.Todd7. Conisford.3).

23 H. M. Cautley, *Suffolk Churches and Their Treasures* (3rd edn, Ipswich, 1954), p. 197.

24 For a 15th-century example of an aumbry door, decorated with the Agnus Dei, see NMS, NWHCM: 1891.50.876. Sometimes all that remains is an enigmatic wall alcove, as at Happisburgh. Occasionally they are found in an aisle, identifying a side chapel with a separate complement of mass vessels.

25 J. Le Goff, *The Birth of Purgatory* (trans. Arthur Goldhammer; Chicago, Ill., 1983). Recent scholarship has qualified Le Goff's chronology.
26 Examples are Chantilly, Musée Condé, 'Les très riches heures du duc de Berry', fol. 113v, and Bad Wimpfen, predella from the high altar in the Stadtkirche. In an anonymous late-16th century portrait of Dante (Washington, National Gallery of Art, Samuel H. Kress Collection 1961.9.57) Dante looks towards the mountain that was Purgatory, supposedly created by the Devil crash landing and punching it up through the Earth!
27 N. Llewellyn, *Funeral Monuments in Post-Reformation England* (Cambridge, 2000), p. 269.
28 NMS, NWHCM: 1956.207.
29 And they continued to turn up: C. R. M. Manning, 'A monumental brass, discovered under the pews in St. Stephen's Church, Norwich', *Norfolk Archaeology*, 6 (1864), pp. 295–9.
30 Blomefield, iv, p. 496n.
31 G. M. Rushforth, *Medieval Christian Imagery* (Oxford, 1936) pp.198–200, writing of Great Malvern Priory.
32 NMS, NWHCM: 1951.168.
33 Local provenance of this piece cannot be demonstrated. Catherine, Barbara and Dorothea all appear with the Virgin and child and Margaret of Antioch – similarly qualified as a resistant virgin – in a painting of c.1516 by Lucas Cranach the elder, 'The Mystical Marriage of St Catherine' (Budapest, Museum of Fine Arts inv.133).
34 Norfolk Museums Service has numerous pilgrim badges of the Virgin, usually of pewter, from across the county. Similar pewterwork sometimes constitutes high-quality compositions: NMS, KILLM: 1978.196.205 (on display in King's Lynn Museum). The discussion here is illustrative rather than exhaustive. A general feature of medieval devotion is its elaboration on an original topic. I have not attempted to distinguish between the large number of Marian sub-themes.
35 See e.g. N. Morgan, 'The Coronation of the Virgin by the Trinity and other texts and images of the glorification of Mary in fifteenth century England', in N. Rogers (ed.), *England in the Fifteenth Century, Proceedings of the 1992 Harlaxton Symposium* (Stamford, Calif., 1994) pp. 223–41.
36 Blomefield, iv, pp. 382n, 385.
37 Blomefield, iv, p. 344.
38 M. Rose, 'The vault bosses', pp. 373–5 in I. Atherton et al. (eds), *Norwich Cathedral: Church, City and Diocese, 1096–1996* (London and Rio Grande, 1996).
39 Blomefield, iv, p. 356. John was a goldsmith and an alderman between 1461 and 1485 (Blomefield, vi, pp. 433–4). More generally, a range of personal devotions is evidenced by the numerous requests in wills to be buried before a specific altar or light.
40 Best seen in the etching by J. S. Cotman (e.g. NMS, NWHCM: 1954.138. Todd 8. Wymer. 86).
41 But not always.
42 The original dedication of the church is to St Mary and Marian elements are to be expected.
43 Blomefield, xi, p. 143.
44 N. Pevsner and B. Wilson, *Norfolk: 1 Norwich and North-East* (London, 1997), p. 668.
45 NMS, NWHCM: 1983.46. See A. Martindale, 'The Ashwellthorpe triptych', pp. 107–23 in D. Williams (ed.), *Early Tudor England: Proceedings of the 1987 Harlaxton Symposium* (Woodbridge, 1989).
46 For example, Potter Heigham, with a primary dedicated to St Nicholas (wall painting); Hingham.
47 Blomefield, iv, p. 239.
48 Blomefield, iv, p. 321.
49 Blomefield, iv, p. 485.

50 There were also colleges of secular priests at the Carnary and at the hospital of St Giles.
51 Its first chaplain said the morning mass of the Virgin before the image of the Virgin at St James's altar; the ninth chaplain was responsible for saying the daily mass of the Blessed Virgin Mary (Blomefield, iv, pp. 171, 173). Appropriately, its seal had at its centre the lily, the cognizance of the Virgin (Blomefield, iv, p. 170).
52 The matching work on the east end of the chancel is a good Victorian restoration.
53 Blomefield, iv, pp. 494–5. It has been suggested that a chantry priest was a desirable post (Tanner, *Church in Norwich*, p. 51), and they did not constitute a clerical underclass.
54 Blomefield, iv, p. 295.
55 Blomefield, iv, pp. 355, 330.
56 Bells normally survived until the craze for change ringing in the 18th century led to the larger older bells being melted down in order to make more tuneful rings. NMS, NWHCM: L1947.146. There was a chapel dedicated to the Virgin at the east end of the south aisle at St James (Blomefield, iv, p. 424).
57 There was one in the south aisle. A statue of the Virgin is documented here, with a candle burning before it (Blomefield, iv, p. 424).
58 Blomefield, iv, p. 179.
59 R. Gilchrist and M. Oliva, *Religious Women in Medieval East Anglia: History and Archaeology c1100–1540* (Norwich, 1993) p. 28; Blomefield, iv, p. 578. Its devotion to the Virgin is reflected in its seal (e.g. 13th-century lead seal purporting to be for Carrow Abbey, engraved with an image of the Virgin Mary and Child and inscribed 'S' SANCTE MARIE IVXTA NORWICV', found at St Paul's Church, Norwich: NMS, NWHCM: 1894.76.175).
60 The Priory was a place of pilgrimage and laid claim to a number of relics (Blomefield, iv, pp. 426–7).
61 For example at East Barsham, where an alabaster fragment of St Anne was recovered, and on the screen at Houghton St Giles which displays the Holy Kindred. Perhaps the emphasis was on Anne as a precursory figure prior to arrival at the shrine to her daughter? Was the Holy Family mapped on to Norfolk's topography in the minds of contemporaries? The road from London passed through Thetford with its Cluniac priory dedicated to the Virgin. A few hundred yards from the priory are the remains of the Priory of the Holy Sepulchre, a house of an order of canons dedicated to aiding pilgrims heading towards Christ's tomb.
62 Blomefield, iv, pp. 154–5; Tanner, *Church in Norwich*, pp. 231–2; D. Harford, 'Richard of Caister, and his metrical prayer', *Norfolk Archaeology*, 17 (1909), pp. 221–44. For local saints and pilgrimages see discussion above of St Leonard's Priory. There was also the cult of St William at the Cathedral, of the Holy Cross at Bromholm and the minor shrines in proximity to Norwich.
63 A surviving undated example from Norfolk depicts the Virgin and Child (NMS NWHCM : 1972.79.3).
64 On display in the small museum in the north transept, and dug up in the churchyard before 1745 (P. Lasko and N. J. Morgan (eds), *Medieval Art in East Anglia 1300–1520*, Norwich, 1973, p. 56). It was the focus of antiquarian interest in the 19th century (see NMS, NWHCM: 1954.138.Todd7.Mancroft.85b; NWHCM: 1951.235.B34).
65 Tanner, *Church in Norwich*, pp. 37–8.
66 R. W. Pfaff, *New Liturgical Feasts in Later Medieval England* (Oxford 1970) p. 129, and more widely his *The Liturgy in Medieval England: A History* (Cambridge, 2009).
67 H. Blake et al., 'From popular devotion to resistance and revival in England: the cult of the holy name of Jesus and the Reformation', pp.175–203 in D. Gaimster and R. Gilchrist (eds), *The Archeology of Reformation 1480–1580* (Leeds, 2003). An early mention of the cult occurs at Sheringham in 1327 (A. E. Nichols, *The Early Art of Norfolk: A Subject List of Extant and Lost Art*

Including Items Relevant to Early Drama, Kalamazoo, Mich., 2002, p. 6). It was depicted in the glass at Salle. For the feast of the name of Jesus see Pfaff, *New Feasts*, pp. 62–83. The occasional combination of the two cults is suggested by the gift of John Withnale in 1503 in support of the daily mass of Jesus and our Lady in St Andrew's, Norwich. (The daily Jesus mass was celebrated in the Lady chapel in the north aisle: Blomefield, iv, p. 304.) In St Gregory's the Jesus mass was celebrated in a secondary Marian chapel of the Assumption at the west end of the tower (Blomefield, iv, p. 273).

68 Blomefield, iv, p. 302.
69 Tanner, *Church in Norwich,* p.103.
70 Blomefield, iv, p. 198.
71 Blomefield, iv, p. 304.
72 In the form 'IHS' (see also p. 000).
73 Blomefield, iv, p. 371.
74 Blomefield, iv, pp. 11, 290.
75 NMS, NWHCM: 1951.235.B101, ink and watercolour depiction by C. J. W. Winter, 1846; NMS NWHCM: 1892.13, Four watercolour drawings, in glazed wooden frames showing original condition of painted panels of the roof of St John Maddermarket (NWHCM: 1892.13) original panels.
76 NMS, NWHCM : 1894.76.1679.
77 Blomefield, iv, p. 225 (the Lamb was briefly renamed the Slug and Lettuce); iv, p.102.
78 Other benefactions to religious institutions by Sir Thomas Erpingham (c.1355–1428) were also markedly heraldic, such as the new east window in the church of the Augustinian Friars in Norwich (DNB). For the heraldry on the gate more generally see T. Simms, 'The Erpingham Gate' pp. 91–6 in A. Curry (ed.), *Agincourt* (Stroud, 2000). This combination of secular and religious heraldry is also to be seen on the 'Erpingham chasuble' (V&A: T.256–1967 and V&A, *Gothic: Art for England 1400–1547*, London, 2003, p. 410, Cat. Item 299). The emblems of Christ were assimilated to the symbolic repertoire of heraldic conventions.
79 Blomefield, iv, p. 55. Cf. M. D. Anderson, *History and Imagery in British Churches* (London, 1971), plate 30. The imagery of the five wounds also appeared on one of the facets of the font in St Peter Southgate (Blomefield, iv, p. 68) and on a monument in the nave of St Andrew's (Blomefield, iv, p. 306).
80 V&A: T.256–1967. This seems to be a particularly English motif.
81 Blomefield, iv, p. 58.
82 It may also have been promoted by the intense piety of certain friars in the city and secular clergy such as Richard Poringland to whom the sufferings of Christ had a special appeal (M. C. Erler, *Women, Reading, and Piety in Late Medieval England*, Cambridge, 2002, pp. 79-80). He was the author of a treatise on the passion of Christ (Blomefield, iv, p. 112).
83 From an anthropological viewpoint totemic objects may be apotropaic in that they shield the owner from evil, or talismanic in that they attract benefits. Of course, in the thinking of many people who hold these beliefs the two functions are likely to merge.
84 NMS NWHCM: 1908.22.133.6. Steps were taken to ensure that the host itself was not removed from the church. However, carrying representations of it in the form of a pilgrim badge might offer protection (NMS, KILLM: 1978.196.177).
85 For some discussion of the investment of sentiment in objects see V. Morgan, 'Presidential Address', 2001.
86 See the illuminated manuscript illustration reproduced in E. Duffy, *Marking the Hours: English People and their Prayers 1240–1570* (New Haven, Conn. and London, 2006), pp. 60–1.
87 Quoted in S. Yaxley, *The Reformation in Norfolk Parish Churches* (Guist, 1990), p. 13. (This is a very useful and practical popular introduction to the topic.)

88 Tanner, *Church in Norwich*, p. 107.
89 Blomefield, iv, p. 89.
90 Blomefield, iv, p. 153.
91 E.g. NMS, NWHCM: 1908.22.133.5). For a representation on a pilgrim badge of the Virgin wearing her girdle see NMS, KILLM: 1978.196.210. Rings could serve the same purpose (e.g. medieval copper alloy ring badge, which would originally have enclosed a fleur-de-lys, the emblem of the Virgin Mary (NMS, NWHCM: 1908.22.133.6). I noted the girdle of the Virgin said to have been owned by the Priory of St Leonard's. As a result of Christ and the Virgin being bodily taken up into heaven only their bodily fluids (blood and milk) or detachable parts (such as hair and teeth) could become relics. As a consequence objects associated with them, such as the wood of the cross and the girdle, became especially sought after. Nowadays the Continent provides examples of what was collected. There is a neatly labelled and remarkably comprehensive display of relics and reliquaries in the Duomo in Bologna.
92 Oxford, Bodleian Library, MS Douce 112, fol. 21r.
93 See M. Champion, *Medieval Graffiti: The Lost Voices of England's Churches* (London, 2015).
94 Champion, *Graffiti*, p. 38; see also p. 134.
95 Thirty-Nine Articles (1563) Article 22.
96 For succinct overviews of the theological debates see A. E. McGrath, *Reformation Thought: An Introduction* (3rd edn, Oxford, 1999) and C. Lindberg (ed.), *The Reformation Theologians: An Introduction to Theology in the Early Modern Period* (Oxford, 2002).
97 In the late 16th century among the godly he was up there in the pantheon of reformist theologians: see e.g. H. C. Porter, *Reformation and Reaction in Tudor Cambridge* (Cambridge, 1958), pp. 345, 359–60.
98 C. Wilkins-Jones (ed.), *The Minutes, Donation Book and Catalogue of Norwich City Library 1608, Founded in 1608* (Norwich, 2008), pp.17–18, 20; F. Kitton (comp.), *Catalogus Librorum Bibliotheca Norvicensi: A Catalogue of the Books in the Free Library of the City of Norwich* (Norwich, 1883), pp. 10–11.
99 This is to be seen throughout the five volumes of his papers published so far: see A. H. Smith and V. Morgan (gen. eds), *The Papers of Nathaniel Bacon of Stiffkey, I–V: 1566–1602* (Norwich, 1978–2000).
100 The oldest surviving bell in the county dates from 1320–40 and comes from Hales. It is now in Lynn Museum (NMS, KILLM: 1974.47).
101 Daily practice among my Muslim acquaintances demonstrates that it is possible to sustain the required devotions even in a secular society. In addition to the bells sounding from the friaries there was a massive detached bell tower in the Cathedral Close, the foundations of which were unearthed during building work in 1956. It would have 'broadcast' monastic time across the City.
102 H. M. Cautley, *Norfolk Churches* (Ipswich, 1949 [1950]), p. 11. This was distinct from the bell rung internally during the service.
103 See also H. M. Cautley, *Suffolk Churches and Their Treasures* (3rd edn, Ipswich, 1954), pp. 43–4.
104 At St Peter Mancroft the east end arch also dealt with the fall of the land from the top of the market. In addition to the west entrance and doorway the rather over-egged tower is also pierced for processional use on the north and south sides. The recent conversion of the east-end arch for social uses is an improvement on its state in the 19th century (see NWHCM: 1894.76.1077). Perceptually and psychologically, parallelism could lead to aspergement being seen as a quasi-person, because the holy water used had been blessed in the water stoup at the entrance to the church, and in the font. The applications of it to people involved entry into the church, both practically and symbolically. Might an asperged church building then enter again into the Church ethereal? In doing so it took the adjacent part of the city into the Christian

geography of a Biblical realm written in terms of the great cities of Jewish and Christian antiquity.
105   Tanner, *Church in Norwich*, p. 37.
106   Discussed more fully in my forthcoming book on civic ritual in Norwich, Renaissance to Enlightenment.
107   Quoted in Tanner, *Church in Norwich*, p. 99.
108   Yaxley, Reformation, p.20.
109   Blomefield, iv, pp. 339, 342.
110   Blomefield, iv, pp. 356, 239.
111   Blomefield, iv, p. 484.
112   Blomefield, iv, pp. 120, 162, 239.
113   Blomefield, iv, pp. 299, 326.
114   Blomefield, iv, p. 473.
115   Blomefield, iv, p. 212. It had religious connotations. This seems to be distinct from the 'main' market cross, which had much earlier origins.
116   Blomefield, iv, pp. 234–5.
117   Blomefield, iv, pp. 286–7.
118   Blomefield, iv, pp. 442, 445.
119   (Gressenhall) Norfolk Historic Environment Record, # 26324.
120   Blomefield, iv, p. 511.
121   Blomefield, iv, p. 130. The building was known as 'the Holy Cross of Bromholm'.
122   Blomefield, iv, p. 117.
123   Blomefield, iv, p. 522.
124   Blomefield, iv, pp.162, 475, 213.
125   W. Henderson, *Notes on the Folk-lore of the Northern Counties of England and the Borders* (2nd edn, London, 1879), p. 80. My late friend Alan Carter, Director of the Norwich Survey, thought the name derived from the Little Cockey, a natural drainage channel that – now in a culvert – runs down the lane, making it especially damp and suited to willows. The two explanations are not incompatible.
126   There was a guild of the Holy Cross that worshipped in the church of the Augustinian canons (Blomefield, iv, p. 90).
127   Blomefield, iv, p. 299.
128   Blomefield, iv, p. 39; for other such dedicatory crosses in the Cathedral, see Blomefield, iv, pp. 40–1.
129   Blomefield, iv, p. 344.
130   Blomefield, iv, p. 36.
131   A. Watkin (ed.), *Inventory of Church Goods temp. Edward III* (Norwich, 1947–8) I, pp.1–3, along with a wide variety of other liturgical objects.
132   Also at Booton, St Margaret Lynn, Attlebridge, and there is implicit evidence for them at Costessey, Diss, Quiddenham, East Ruston, Great Melton, Sustead and Bromholm Priory (Nichols, *Art*, pp. 77, 78, 86, 132, 139). Also depicted in a wall painting at Potter Heigham and the screen at Worstead (Nichols, *Art*, pp. 248–9, 313.).
133   Even in the early 18th century Blomefield felt the need to explain that they had been processional entry points (Blomefield, iv, p. 524).
134   On the south porch, as the church lacks a west door.
135   This was an adoption of the more elaborate services on Palm Sunday in cathedrals (see P. Draper, 'Architecture and liturgy', p. 86 in J. Alexander and P. Binski (eds), *Age of Chivalry: Art in Plantagenet England 1200–1400*, London, 1987).
136   Red velvet with gold, green, yellow and white stitching, in the centre the Virgin is borne up

by angels and flanked by seraphim; other decorative devices include foliage, fleurs-de-lis (itself the insignia of the Virgin), rayed suns and double-headed birds; the motifs are embroidered on linen and applied to a red silk velvet cope (NMS, NWHCM: 1939.75). Given the evidence of 19th-century Anglo-Catholic activity at Burnham Deepdale, its 15th-century Rhenish chasuble may be a later importation. Numerous vestments are mentioned in the inventories of church goods drawn up in 1552. These require more detailed analysis than can be provided here.

137 V&A: T.256–1967.
138 Practice in the positioning of the priest in the Mass changed over time. According to one view in the early-medieval period he officiated behind the altar, facing the congregation This is highly debatable, and probably not true. After the Reformation he faced the altar with his back to the congregation. Recent changes in the Catholic church mean the celebrant now faces the congregation while standing in front of the altar.
139 Screens have attracted a great deal of attention from art historians because they often have some of the earliest surviving forms of panel painting. See e.g. J. Mitchell, 'Painting in East Anglia around 1500: the continental connection', pp.365-80 in J. Mitchell and M. Moran (eds), *England and the Continent in the Middle Ages: Studies in Memory of Andrew Martindale – Proceedings of the 1996 Harlaxton Symposium* (Stamford, Calif., 2000); P. Plummer, 'The Ranworth Rood Screen', pp. 292–5 in 'Report of the Summer Meeting of the Royal Archaeological Institute at Norwich in 1979', *Archaeological Journal,* 137 (1979); B. Camm, 'Some Norfolk rood-screens', pp. 237–95 in Clement Ingleby (ed. and intro.), *A Supplement to Blomefield's Norfolk* (London, 1929); S. Cotton, 'Mediaeval rood screens in Norfolk – their construction and painting dates', *Norfolk Archaeology,* 40 (1987) pp. 44–54; for an excellent brief discussion see A. E. Nichols, *The Early Art of Norfolk: A Subject List of Extant and Lost Art Including Items Relevant to Early Drama* (Kalamazoo, Mich., 2002), pp. 321–2.
140 The screen at Harling is made up of four distinct segments. I am indebted to my friend David King for the elucidation of all things to do with Harling.
141 Art historians vary, but mostly take them to come from the rood screen (A. Moore and M. Thøfner (eds), *The Art of Faith: 3,500 Years of Art and Belief in Norfolk,* London, 2010, p. 30, and V&A cataloguing). Others think they came from the chapel of St Mary (Lasko and Morgan, *Medieval Art in East Anglia 1300–1520,* pp. 50, 51).
142 Blomefield, iv, p. 344.
143 Blomefield's description of Blackfriars based on then-extant sources evokes a good sense of the crowded character of this building: iv, p. 344.
144 The original version of this paper was delivered in St Edmunds, Fishergate. As a redundant church it has yet again found new uses, as it did in the 16th century. See Blomefield, iv, p. 405. Quite a few local sites of specific devotion do not make it on to the pilgrimage 'A' list, including St Walstan at Bawburgh, St John's head at Trimingham, the sword of Winfarthing, St Albert of Cringleford, and Our Lady of Pity at Horstead (Yaxley, *Reformation,* p.20). They continued to receive offerings in the early 16th century. The texts associated with Wulstan encouraged his devotees to invoke his intercessory role (E. Duffy, *The Stripping of the Altars: Traditional Religion in England 1400–1580,* New Haven, Conn. and London, 1992, pp. 200–5).
145 NWHCM : 1935.130, oil on panel. Inscribed 'Mr. Henry Birde prcher / AO. DNI. 1583 / AETATIS.SUE. 60 / spero sed no spiro'.
146 The Injunctions of 1538 required all parishes to purchase a copy. More than 9,000 copies had been printed by 1541.
147 These boards are difficult to examine as they are now hung. They appear to have been repainted, possibly a number of times. Are they on the reverse of part of a doom that had hung over the tympanum? Given how little material culture of the immediate post-reformation survives it

148 V. Morgan, 'Cambridge University and "the country" 1540–1640', pp. 239–42 in L. Stone (ed.), *The University in Society* (1974, 1975).
149 M. I. Fewster, 'East Anglian goldsmiths: dimensions of a craft community, 1500–1750' (UEA PhD, 2004).
150 Quoted in H. C. Porter, *Reformation and Reaction in Tudor Cambridge* (Cambridge, 1958), p. 121.
151 P. Collinson, *The Elizabethan Puritan Movement* (London, 1967), pp. 71–83, 92–7.
152 V. Morgan, J. Key and B. Taylor (eds), *The Papers of Nathaniel Bacon of Stiffkey, IV: 1596–1602* (Norwich, 2000), pp. xliv–xlv, 64–5.
153 Collinson, *The Elizabethan Puritan Movement* pp. 186; John More, *Three Godly and Frutifull Sermons* (Cambridge, 1594) STC2 18074.5, quotation from the 'Epistle' by Nicholas Bownd.
154 Quoted in Yaxley, *Reformation in Norfolk Parish Churches*, p.15, and pp.16, 46.
155 By Cornelius Jansson Walter Winter (1821–1891), a well-known 19th-century antiquarian artist. Watercolour on paper, undated (NMS, NWHCM: 1894.76.1231).
156 V. Morgan, 'Some types of patronage, mainly in sixteenth- and seventeenth-century England', pp. 91–116 in A. Maczak (ed.), *Klientelsysteme Im Europa der Fruhen Neuzeit* (Munich, 1988).
157 It is typical of the treatment of post-Reformation features in churches that the wall paintings at West Walton receive short shrift (cf. D. P. Mortlock, and C. V. Roberts, *The Guide to Norfolk Churches*, Cambridge, 2007, pp. 313–14). In addition there is evidence of an early, 13th-century painted decorative scheme (NMS, NWHCM: 1954.138. Todd 19. Freebridge.146, 'Paintings from the Clerestory and Spandril, West Walton Church', coloured lithograph on paper, 1847. The painting is still in situ).
158 Moore and Thøfner, T*he Art of Faith*, pp. 52–3, with illustration.
159 See e.g. NMS, NWHCM: 1894.76.435.2. There is a full examination in V. Morgan, 'Perambulating and consumable emblems: the Norwich evidence', pp. 167–206 in M. Bath and D. Russell (eds), *Deviceful Settings: The English Renaissance Emblem and Its Contexts: Selected Papers from the Third International Emblem Conference, Pittsburgh, 1993* (New York, 1999); see also V. Morgan, 'A ceremonious society: an aspect of institutional power in early modern Norwich', pp. 133–63 in A. Goldgar and R. I. Frost (eds), *Institutional Culture in Early Modern Society* (Leiden, Netherlands and Boston, Mass., 2004) ; D. Ezzy, G. Easthope and V. Morgan, 'Ritual dynamics: mayor making in early modern Norwich', *Journal of Historical Sociology*, 22, 2009, pp. 396–419. The Tudor 'dynasticization' of churches is a larger topic that cannot be explored fully here.
160 G. W. O. Addleshaw and F. Etchells, *The Architectural Setting of Anglican Worship* (London, 1948) pp. 22–36; N. Yates, *Buildings, Faith and Worship: The Liturgical Arrangement of Anglican Churches 1600–1900* (Oxford, 2000).
161 Yaxley, *Reformation*, p. 42.
162 In design it is not dissimilar to the 'holy table' at North Walsham, although far rougher in finish. Both conform to the general requirements for these tables.
163 G. Parry, *Glory, Laud and Honour: The Arts of the Anglican Counter-Reformation* (Woodbridge, 2006).
164 J. Maltby, *Prayer Book and People in Elizabethan and Early Stuart England* (Cambridge, 1998); D. MacCulloch, *The Later Reformation in England, 1547–1603* (Basingstoke, 2001).
165 The most complete furnishings of a parish church in Norfolk of this period are in Wilby, which was refitted after a fire of 1633.
166 Matthew Reynolds, *Godly Reformers and Their Opponents in Early Modern England: Religion in Norwich, c.1560–1643* (Woodbridge, 2005).

Norwich's Catholic chapels

Francis Young

Norwich is a city renowned for its dissenting religious tradition, but its history as a Catholic city is perhaps less well known, at least before the construction of the magnificent Church (now Cathedral) of St John the Baptist in the 1890s. As John Bossy argued in the 1970s, Catholicism before the restoration of the English hierarchy of bishops in 1850 was 'a variety of nonconformity',[1] and nowhere more so than in Norwich, where some of the most outspoken advocates of social change in the early 19th century were Catholics. The focus of this paper is the Catholic chapels of Norwich, but in order to approach this subject it is necessary to understand something about the composition of Norwich's Catholic community.

Norwich's Catholic chapels have been examined before, first in the handsome volume produced to mark the completion of the church of St John the Baptist (now the Catholic Cathedral) in 1913, *A Great Gothic Fane*, subtitled *A retrospect of Catholicity in Norwich*, which was largely the work of J. W. Picton.[2] An important contribution was later made by the great Jesuit historian Geoffrey Holt in his 1979 article on 'Catholic chapels in Norwich before 1900' in *Norfolk Archaeology*.[3] Holt subsequently edited some of the correspondence of Fr Edward Galloway, the Jesuit priest in Norwich in the 1760s and 1770s.[4] Finally, the history of the old chapels was ably summarized by Anthony Rossi in his 1998 article on the building history of the Cathedral of St John the Baptist.[5]

Roman Catholicism was a religion formally proscribed by law in England between 1559 and 1778, when the First Catholic Relief Act allowed Catholics to serve as officers in the British Army. The Second Catholic Relief Act of 1791 finally legalized the celebration of mass in privately owned Catholic chapels, and in 1829 Catholics were awarded full civil and political rights. Strictly speaking all Catholic churches in England had the status of chapels until 1917, when the bishops of England and Wales established parishes. However, although chapels were only legal

Figure 1 *A Great Gothic Fane*

Figure 2 The Duke's Palace, Norwich (taken from Picton, 1913)

after 1791 this does not mean they did not exist, and in Norwich there is evidence of illegal Catholic chapels from the 1650s onwards.

The Catholic community in post-Reformation Norwich

On or before 24 June 1559 the last legal mass was said in Norwich's myriad ancient churches, as the Act of Uniformity in Public Worship came into force and replaced the Latin Use of Sarum with the plain ceremonies of the English Prayer Book. However, we know that at least as many English people opposed the religious changes as supported them, and many clergy were likewise hostile to the Reformation. Priests ordained in the reigns of Henry VIII and Mary continued to minister alongside protestant clergy ordained in the reigns of Edward VI and Elizabeth, and some offered the mass (illegally) as an alternative to the authorized service. Still others, some of them former chantry priests and some of them priests ejected from their offices for refusing to swear the Oath of Supremacy to Elizabeth, formed an underground network of priests who said mass in private houses.

We know little about the early days of underground Catholics in Norwich, except that the palace of the dukes of Norfolk, which was built some time after 1563, provided a refuge for religious conservatives. In 1565 William Allen stayed at the palace before leaving for the Continent, where he would go on to found colleges to train English priests at Douai and Rouen, eventually becoming cardinal protector of England in 1587.[6] Indeed, the Duke's Palace was a focus of Catholic activity in Norwich even after 1710, when it ceased to be a ducal residence. The duke's ownership of the building meant that the bishop of Norwich had no powers of visitation. The law permitted peers of the realm complete control over their

Figure 3 Costessey Hall (taken from Picton, 1913)

own private chapels, and although in theory these had to be protestant, peers were protected from arbitrary searches of their property in a way that others were not. Most historians have assumed that a chapel existed somewhere in the Duke's Palace and that mass would have been said there in the 16th and 17th centuries, although direct evidence is lacking.

Recusancy (refusal to attend church – a crime after 1559) was rife in Norfolk in the 1560s and 1570s, and Catholic sympathies ran high, especially among the gentry but also among the ordinary people. In 1570 Sir John Appleyard, who had served as sheriff of Norfolk in Mary's reign, successfully whipped up a riot in Norwich against the 'Strangers', Dutch protestant refugees to whom Elizabeth's government gave refuge from the Spanish. Although the motive of most of the rioters was purely xenophobic, Appleyard's was religious, and one of his closest allies was Edmund Harcocke, the former Dominican prior. Appleyard and Harcocke hoped that popular rejection of the Strangers, who were allowed their own protestant services in their own language, would lead to the rejection of protestantism altogether, as had happened in Durham when, in 1569, rebels occupied the city and restored the mass in the cathedral.[7]

The East Anglian gentry seemed to lack the stomach for rebellion, however, and when the disgraced duke of Norfolk rode to Kenninghall in 1572 no one rallied to him as they had to Queen Mary in 1553. In 1578 Elizabeth came on a progress through East Anglia, with Norwich as her final destination, in order to impose the protestant Reformation once and for all. Outwardly, the progress was all courtesy and glamour, but its real purpose was to test the loyalty of Elizabeth's Catholic subjects. Famously, when the queen rode into Norwich, she looked down at a group of curtseying children and said 'I know you do not love me here.'[8] In the weeks and months after the progress there was an official crackdown on recusants, and many Norfolk Catholics were fined and imprisoned.

After the attainder of the fourth duke of Norfolk in 1572 temporarily reduced the influence of the Howard family in the nation at large and in Norwich, another less exalted but equally committed Catholic family stepped into the breach locally, the Jerninghams of Costessey. The Jerninghams belonged to that hard core of recusants whose loyalty

Figure 4 The attic chapel at Costessey Hall (from Picton, 1913)

to the Catholic faith stemmed from their involvement in Queen Mary's regime in the years 1553–58. Sir Henry Jerningham, who died in 1572, was one of the architects in East Anglia of Mary's successful bid for the throne, and was immediately appointed to Mary's Privy Council, serving as vice-chamberlain of the Queen's household, captain of the Queen's Guard, and master of the horse. His greatest disappointment was his failure to defend Calais against the French in 1558. Needless to say, Sir Henry was stripped of his honours at the accession of Elizabeth and retired to his estate just outside Norwich, where he and his successors nurtured the survival of the Catholic faith.

We know frustratingly little of where Catholics worshipped at this early period; it seems almost certain that they did so at Costessey Hall, and in such a large city as Norwich there must surely have been houses where mass was said in secret. It is unsurprising that no evidence survives, as this was an exceedingly dangerous time for priests. In 1616 one of them, Thomas Benstead, was hanged, drawn and quartered in Norwich, and his quarters displayed on St Benedict's Gate. The earliest indication we have of any regularized Catholic mission in Norwich comes from the 1650s, when the Jesuits arrived.

The early Jesuit mission, c. 1647–1725

Since 1633, the Jesuits in East Anglia and Essex had been organized into the College of the Holy Apostles, which was founded by the influential Petre family. The college was not a physical building but a body of priests under a superior, who formed part of the larger

Jesuit mission in England. During the civil war and interregnum the Catholic Church in England was run by the Chapter of the Secular Clergy, which was left behind when a bishop appointed by the pope, Richard Smith, was forced to leave the country in 1635. The chapter was led at the time by a priest who was a fierce critic of the Jesuits, Thomas White, who controversially advocated the Holy See's recognition of the regime of Oliver Cromwell. White was also a controversial theologian, and wrote against the traditional Catholic understanding of the doctrine of purgatory. He was answered in print by the Norfolk-born Jesuit James Mumford, in a book entitled *The Remembrance for the Living to Pray for the Dead*. For Mumford, as for many English Catholics, prayer for the souls in purgatory was a touchstone of the Catholic faith and one of the markers that distinguished Catholics from protestants.

The earliest Jesuit priest recorded to have been in Norwich was Francis Sankey in 1647.[9] In 1650 Mumford was ordered to leave his position as rector of the Jesuit College at Liege and sent to Norwich, where he was rector of the College of the Holy Apostles by 1655. This suggests that Norwich was at this time the epicentre of the Jesuit mission in East Anglia. We know that Mumford maintained some sort of chapel, as in 1658 he was arrested and paraded around Norwich in priest's vestments, accompanied by soldiers with altar vessels dangling from their spears. This suggests that a secret chapel was raided at the time Mumford was arrested. Mumford was taken to Great Yarmouth to be imprisoned, but managed to negotiate his return to Norwich. He was released from prison after some months, but the incident forced the Jesuits to move their headquarters out of Norwich and back to the countryside, although we do not know exactly where.[10]

In 1676 the bishop of London, Henry Compton, organized a census of religious worship throughout England, including the diocese of Norwich, which asked incumbents to return numbers of conformists, nonconformists and papists in each parish. Out of a total of 10,542 people recorded in Norwich, 9,994 (95 per cent) attended their parish church on Sundays. There were 449 people recorded as nonconformists (4.7 per cent of the total) and only 49 as papists (0.5 per cent).[11] On the face of it, the evidence of the Compton census is that Catholics were a vanishingly marginal group in 17th-century Norwich, but there are reasons to believe that this evidence is not as reliable as it seems.

It seems unlikely that there were as few as 10,000 communicants in Norwich in 1676, and therefore it is probable that heads of household only were being counted. Furthermore, the data was collected by incumbents, who were in a good position to know how many conformists there were in their parish, but may have had little more than rumour and conjecture to go on when it came to nonconformists and Catholics. A large papist population would have been an embarrassment to most incumbents, and because incumbents were required only to give numbers rather than names, it is possible that some clergy deliberately underestimated numbers. Add to this the fact that in 1676 some Catholics may still have practised 'occasional conformity', deliberately attending a minimal number of protestant services in the parish church to avoid indictment for recusancy. It is therefore likely that there were considerably more than 49 people in Norwich in 1676 who would have identified themselves as Catholics.

In 1679 another Jesuit, Nathaniel Stafford, was arrested at Norwich.[12] This was at the height of the so-called 'Popish Plot', an episode of national hysteria that led to the arrest, imprisonment and even execution of dozens of Catholic priests and laymen. However, the storm was soon followed by a break in the clouds when, in 1685, Charles II was succeeded by his Catholic brother James, duke of York. Under James II Catholics became bolder than ever before, and the Jesuit College of the Holy Apostles purchased a permanent headquarters in the Abbot's Palace in the abbey ruins at Bury St Edmunds. Nathaniel Stafford, whose brother John became the new mayor of Bury, played a key role in the foundation of the new Jesuit chapel and school.[13]

Even though Bury rather than Norwich was now the centre of the Jesuit mission, Catholics in Norwich were also emboldened. Three Catholics, James Hacon, Charles Skinner and William Cobb, petitioned the Court of Mayoralty for the use of the chancel of the old Dominican Priory of St Andrew, which had previously been used by Dutch protestants. The petition was refused, but after a further request from Sir Henry Bedingfield in 1687 the Court of Mayoralty granted the Jesuits the use of the western granary of the old priory, which was leased to them for 12 pence a year. This building may have been part of the original kitchen of the old friary, and the chapel was located above the sealing hall, where the crown seal was kept. The chapel was opened on 11 December 1687, when mass was celebrated by Fr Thomas Acton; the chapel was served by him and three other priests, Charles Gage, Robert Petre and William Petre.[14]

The Jesuit chapel was short-lived, and in October 1688 James II was forced to backtrack on his promise to introduce toleration for dissenters and Catholics. The result was a breakdown of law and order, and attacks directed against Catholic chapels, including the one in Norwich. On 14 October the mayor and sheriffs managed to disperse a mob that had gathered to attack the chapel, but once news reached Norwich of the prince of Orange's invasion, on 7 and 8 December the mob pulled down the chapel and burned all its furnishings. Acton was sent into hiding, but he seems to have stayed in Norwich until 1692.

What happened next is obscure. In 1713 a Jesuit called Richard Cotton was certainly in Norwich, but there are two different traditions about where he lived and had his chapel. According to Frederick Husenbeth, writing in the 1860s, the Jesuit chapel relocated to Shoulder of Mutton Yard, but the Catholic printer and publisher William Eusebius Andrews was convinced that the Jesuits were based at the Hare and Hounds in Chapelfields. Andrews, as a native of Norwich, was probably in a better position to know the truth than Husenbeth, and we know for a fact that the chapel was located in Chapelfields, close to the site of the present Catholic Cathedral, as early as 1725, so the Chapelfields tradition seems most likely to be true.[15]

The Duke's Place chapel, 1721–86

It is in the 1720s that we have the first definitive evidence for a chapel run by secular clergy (priests who belonged to no religious order) in the Duke's Palace. The palace, which had been extensively renovated in 1672, was largely pulled down in 1711, leaving only the offices and outbuildings on the east and north-east sides. What remained was known as the Duke's Place, and the first priest to be stationed there was Fr Ferdinand Silver, who came from Costessey to Norwich in 1721. It is highly likely that priests were stationed at the palace before that date, but no record of them survives. Between 1753 and 1756 the Palace's most famous chaplain was Fr Alban Butler, author of the famous *Lives of the Saints*, who also acted as vicar general for the area and attempted to impose the will of the bishop, who was based in far-away Staffordshire. Butler posed as tutor to Edward Howard,

Figure 5 Interior of the Duke's Place chapel (from Picton, 1913)

the eldest son of the duke of Norfolk.

In 1758 Butler described the Duke's Place to the priest who succeeded him as chaplain, Edward Beaumont:

> The Duke's Place as it is called is a building which his Grace keeps in his own hands and which you have all to yourself. You have a great deal of room … for kitchen, brewing &c … a good stable, though have no occasion for a horse …. The Duke's allowance is 35 pds a year and 10 pds to be given by you among the poor at your discretion, all paid half-yearly by the steward, who is Mr. Havers at Thelton …. There are in the place also things you want and a good collection of books for y[ou]r purpose with a great many that are old-fashioned and useless to you.

In 1764 the Duke built a new house and chapel for Beaumont, but in 1786 the 11th duke

Figure 6 Alban Butler. From *Lives of the Saints* (London, 1956–59), 4 vols.

conformed to the Church of England, and Beaumont and his congregation were forced to decamp to three garret rooms in Willow Lane.[16]

The Second Catholic Relief Act, 1791

In 1759 another Jesuit, Fr Edward Galloway, arrived in Norwich and established himself in St Swithin's Lane, Chapelfields. Between 1758 and 1762 Galloway presided over the construction of a chapel at the northern end of the west side of St Swithin's or Ten Bell Lane. The chapel and house cost at least £1,000. However, neither Galloway nor the Jesuits were able to own the chapel, and it was not until 1791 that the chapel was able to pass into the ownership of Galloway's successor, Fr Thomas Angier. The change in the law also emboldened Beaumont to seek a new home for his secular mission; accordingly, he purchased the so-called 'Dancing Master's Estate' at the back of Stranger's Hall, located off St John's Alley. By 1794 the chapel of St John, Maddermarket had opened, and in 1797 Strangers Hall became the priest's residence. By 1836 the chapel was complemented by a Catholic school.[17]

The Maddermarket chapel was woefully inadequate in size, even when galleries were installed. In the late 18th century Norwich had the second largest Catholic population of any city in the Midland District, which was a vast ecclesiastical jurisdiction covering East Anglia and most of the Midlands. On 3 July 1768, on one of his rare visits to East Anglia, Bishop John Joseph Hornyold confirmed 181 people in Norwich; the only city in his jurisdiction where there were more confirmations was Wolverhampton.[18] In 1767 another government-sponsored census of papists revealed that there were 441 Catholics in total in Norwich, over a third (34 per cent) of all Catholics in East Anglia, and showing considerable growth since the Compton census almost a century earlier (the 1767 census was also a lot more accurate than the earlier count).[19] Next to Bury St Edmunds, Norwich had the highest concentration of Catholics of any town in the region.

By 1793 the Catholic community in East Anglia had begun receiving refugees from the French Revolution, both French nationals and English Catholics from the Continental religious houses. The French priests gave a much needed boost to the Catholic Church in England, but they had to support themselves as best they could since the Catholic Church in England was so poor. One of them, the priest Thomas d'Etreville, earned his living teaching French, Italian and Spanish. One of his pupils was the young George Borrow, although Borrow's rabidly anti-Catholic attitude in his later writings would suggest that d'Etreville did not leave a good impression. In 1800 the first nuns arrived in Norwich since the Reformation, an English community from Paris called the Blue Nuns, who lived in the city under the protection of the Jerningham family.

Owing to the poverty of the Catholic community in Norwich, things remained unchanged until 1823, with a secular chapel at Maddermarket and a Jesuit mission in Chapelfields. In that year the Jesuit priest Fr James Carr petitioned both the Jesuit province and the Catholic bishop, John Milner, for permission to build a new chapel to meet demand. However, the first stone was not laid until 10 August 1827. The new Chapel of the Holy Apostles in Willow Lane, while certainly modest by later standards, was the first Catholic chapel in Norwich designed by an architect, James Patience, and whose purpose was obvious from the public street. Appropriately enough, its completion coincided with Catholic emancipation in 1829. The old chapel in Ten Bell Lane became a school.[20]

Figure 7 The Maddermarket Chapel (photo by the author)

Amalgamation of the missions, 1881–1913

In 1878 the 15th duke of Norfolk first mooted the idea of funding a new church to replace the Maddermarket chapel. The following year a site was purchased at the corner of Earlham Road and Unthank Road where a gaol had previously stood. Both the bishop of Northampton – in whose diocese Norwich was located – and the Jesuits expressed concern that the new site was located so close to Willow Lane, but after protracted negotiations the Jesuits eventually agreed to withdraw from Norwich altogether in order to allow the two mission congregations – St John's, Maddermarket and Holy Apostles, Willow Lane – to be amalgamated in a single church. On 27 January 1881 the Jesuits finally left, and the foundation stone of the new church of St John the Baptist, named after the old Maddermarket chapel, was laid in 1882. It was not until 1894 that the nave of the new church was completed and the congregation was able to move out of the old chapel.[21] The church they moved to, which was finally consecrated in 1913, is arguably the finest example of Early English neo-gothic in Britain and one of the largest Catholic churches then in existence in the country. It was certainly no surprise when this cathedral-sized church was selected for the enthronement of the first bishop of the new Diocese of East Anglia on 3 June 1976. It is now the mother church of all East Anglian Catholics as well as a worthy addition to Norwich's great architectural heritage.

Dr Francis Young *is volumes editor for the Catholic Record Society and the author of many books and articles on Catholicism in East Anglia, most recently* The Gages of Hengrave and

Figure 8 Willow Lane Chapel (photo by the author)

Suffolk Catholicism. *He is currently editing the official history of the Roman Catholic Diocese of East Anglia,* Catholic East Anglia, *for publication in 2016. His book* The Abbey of Bury St Edmunds: History, Legacy and Discovery *will be published by the Lasse Press in 2016.*

Notes

1. John Bossy, *The English Catholic Community, 1570–1850* (London: Longman, 1975), p. 5.
2. [J. W. Picton], *A Great Gothic Fane: The Catholic Church of St. John the Baptist, Norwich, with Historical Retrospect of Catholicity in Norwich* (Norwich: W. T. Pike, 1913).
3. Geoffrey Holt, 'Catholic chapels in Norwich before 1900', *Transactions of the Norfolk & Norwich Archaeological Society* 37 (1979), pp. 153–68.
4. Geoffrey Holt, 'Some letters from Suffolk, 1763–80: selection and commentary', *Recusant History* 16 (1983), pp. 304–15.
5. Anthony Rossi, *Norwich Roman Catholic Cathedral: A Building History* (London: Chapels Society, 1998).
6. Eamon Duffy, 'Allen, William (1532–1594)', *Oxford Dictionary of National Biography*, Oxford

Figure 9 Cathedral of St John the Baptist, Norwich: a painting by S. M. Nichols

University Press, 2004; online edn, Oct 2008 (www.oxforddnb.com/view/article/391, accessed 18 October 2015).

7 M. Reynolds, *Godly Reformers and their Opponents in Early Modern England: Religion in Norwich, c. 1560–1643* (Woodbridge: Boydell, 2005), pp. 56–7.
8 Bernardino Mendoza to Gabriel de Zayas, 8 September 1578, *Calendar of Letters and State Papers relating to English Affairs: preserved principally in the Archives of Simancas,* ed. M. A. S. Hume (London: HMSO, 1892–99), vol. 2, p. 524.
9 Holt (1979), p. 156.
10 Joy Rowe, 'Mumford, James (c.1606–1666)', *Oxford Dictionary of National Biography*, Oxford University Press, 2004 (www.oxforddnb.com/view/article/19525, accessed 18 October 2015).
11 Ann Whiteman and Mary Clapinson (eds), *The Compton Census of 1676: A Critical Edition* (London: British Academy, 1986), pp. 218–19.
12 Holt (1979), p. 156.
13 Francis Young, '"An horrid popish plot": the failure of Catholic aspirations in Bury St Edmunds, 1685–88', *Proceedings of the Suffolk Institute of Archaeology and History* 41 (2006), pp. 209–25.
14 Holt (1979), p. 156.
15 Ibid., pp. 157–8.
16 Ibid., pp. 153–4.
17 Ibid., pp. 158–62.
18 Michael Gandy (ed.), *The Bishops' Register of Confirmations in the Midland District of the Catholic Church in England, 1768–1811 and 1816* (London: Catholic Family History Society, 1999), pp. 1–8.
19 E. S. Worrall (ed.), *Returns of Papists, 1767: Dioceses of England and Wales except Chester* (London: Catholic Record Society, 1989), pp. 125–7.
20 Holt (1979), p. 162.
21 Ibid., pp. 163–5.

'The sheep hath paid for all': church building and self-expression in the Late Middle Ages

Allan B. Barton

In Nottinghamshire, close to the market town of Newark, is an isolated hamlet situated at the very end of a road that leads to nowhere except to the eastern bank of the river Trent. This little hamlet, Holme, contains the church of St Giles, one of the most rewarding church buildings in the East Midlands. St Giles is an example of a church that was entirely rebuilt in a single phase through the efforts of one man, who has left behind his indelible mark upon the place. Because of its isolated location the church was little used and long neglected. It narrowly escaped a thorough restoration by Sir George Gilbert Scott in 1867 and was gently conserved in the 1932 by R. Harley-Smith under the auspices of the Society for the Protection of Ancient Buildings.[1] Many of its late medieval fittings and furnishings, woodwork, glass and stone still survive relatively unscathed, to tell their story and the story of their benefactor.

The benefactor was a man called John Barton, who died in 1491. Barton was a self-made man, a wool merchant who rose from apparent obscurity to create a wool production and export business, which placed him at the very top of his trade. He was a merchant of the

Figure 1 Holme by Newark church from the south,east, showing the Barton Chapel to the right and the porch added by Barton on the left. (Photo by Gordon Plumb.)

Staple of Calais, one of a closed group of wool merchants who had the monopoly in the late Middle Ages on the export of English wool to the continent, and also fixed prices. In due course John Barton reached the very pinnacle of the Staple, serving by his own admission as its mayor, the head of the company and also effective governor of Calais.

Considering that he rose so far in his trade, we know surprisingly little of John Barton's origins. The first time we hear of him in the public record is in 1454, when he and his fellow wool Staplers are ordered to pay a fine to the duke of Burgundy. At this point in his career he was based in Hull.[2] His will tells us that he was married to a woman called Isabella, and if the arms impaled with his own in Holme church are any indicator, it would appear that she was a member of the Bingham family, an ancient but minor Nottinghamshire gentry family.[3] On that basis it is possible his origins were in the East Midlands, but that is pure supposition.

The next time we hear of Barton is in 1472, when he was included in a general pardon of Staple merchants granted by Edward IV as he was returned to the throne after the battle of Tewkesbury. At that time Barton was resident in Holme by Newark, but it is clear that he had only recently established himself there, as he was referred to as 'late' (that is, recently) 'farmer' (the tenant) of the manor of 'Egyll, county Lincoln'.[4] When he made his will in 1490, he referred to his connections to Eagle (as it is spelled today), and asks for the return there of a borrowed liturgical book, a Gradual.[5] His will suggests that he had quite broad landholdings at the time of his death in 1491, and that right up to the end he was in the process of increasing his holdings. There are bequests of property in the neighbouring town of Newark, but also of land in Kent and on the continent, and there are references to recently purchased property in North Muskham, the parish of which Holme forms a part.[6] It seems that at some time between the 1470s and 1480s, when he was already of advanced age and had three generations of descendants, he settled at Holme, and began consciously to use the proceeds of his business to build up a landed estate. The choice to centre that new estate at Holme by Newark was almost certainly a hard-nosed business decision. Holme was located close to the important trading town of Newark and on the banks of the river Trent, a major trade link to Hull and on to the continent.

Having settled on Holme as his base and having begun to construct an estate, like self-made men of all generations, Barton built himself a new house there. Sadly it has since been demolished, but Thoroton, a Nottinghamshire antiquary, saw the house in the 1660s and described it as a 'fair stone house'. Thoroton tells us that it had glazed windows, which incorporated the inscription in many places, 'I thanke God and ever shall the sheep hath paid for all.' This was a feature that underlined to all who saw it, including his descendants who would enjoy a more elevated social status among the gentry, that the Barton family fortune was created through God's blessing and on the back of John Barton's own sheer hard graft and business acumen.[7]

Having built this house and being in the final few years of his life, Barton then turned his attention to the church that stood hard by it. In the early 1480s the church of St Giles Holme, was a modest chapel of ease to the parish church at North Muskham on the other bank of the Trent. It is clear from examining the present structure that building was for much of the Middle Ages a very simple three-cell building, with an aisle-less nave of the 13th century (windowless on the north side), a small chancel of a similar date and a slightly later west tower with a tiny broach spire, a miniature version of the spire at nearby Newark.

During the 1480s John Barton doubled the church in size and renovated the existing fabric. On the south side of the nave he added a new arcade and south aisle. To this he added a south porch, with stair turret and parvise over it, which originally towered over the shallow pitch of the nave aisle. The west tower was given a makeover, with a new west window and tower arch inserted, and new buttresses. The chancel was completely refenestrated and a two-bay south arcade was inserted. This arcade provided entry to a large new south chapel, which we know from the will of John Barton's grandson, also a John, was the 'chapell' of 'our ladye'.[8] This chapel, which is referred to in John Barton's will of 1490 'as the new chapel he has constructed', is a foot wider than the chancel. A Perpendicular glass house, it is lit by three enormous four-light windows.[9] This new south chapel has a higher parapet level than the nave aisle and chancel, standing out prominently. The retained elements of the former building, such as the west tower and chancel with their new buttresses and fenestration, were covered in roughcast to give the visual impression of a unified construction. Thankfully because of the lack of Victorian restoration, some of that roughcast still remains. The newly constructed work – porch, aisle and Lady chapel – was built of coursed ashlar, which would have made it stand out further from the rest of the structure. The north side of the nave, not visible from Barton's house or from the road, was given new buttresses and was covered in roughcast, but was left windowless – there was no need for display where it would not be seen.

Inside the building, the new chapel of Our Lady was divided from the south nave aisle and the chancel by light parclose screens, which remain in situ. The rood screen, identical in form to the parclose screens, also remains.

Under the eastern arch of the south chancel arcade, occupying the space between the high altar and the altar of Our Lady, is John Barton's tomb, the only monument in the church and forming the centrepiece of his new work. The tomb was constructed before his death, for in his will he requests burial in 'novo monumenta in capella per

Figure 2 The monument of John Barton, taken from the Barton Chapel and looking towards the high altar. (Photo by Allan Barton.)

Figure 3 The effigies of John and Isabella Barton. (Photo by Allan Barton.)

me noviter in Holme constructa' (in the new monument in the chapel I have newly built in Holme).[10] Barton's tomb is of a type that was quite avant garde at the time of its construction, a transi tomb. On the upper part of the monument are recumbent effigies of himself and his wife, and below in a vaulted opening is a stone representation of Barton's own elderly corpse in its winding sheet, emaciated and semi-skeletal. Along the base supporting the cadaver is a Latin quote from Job 19, verse 21: 'Have pity on me, have pity on me, you my friends; for the hand of the lord has touched me.' Unusually for a monument of this date, the effigies above appear to be an attempt at portraiture. Barton is portrayed as an elderly man at the height of his wealth and prestige, his great wealth alluded to by the oversize and perhaps slightly ludicrous purse hanging at his waist.

There is no inscription on the tomb except for the scriptural quote, but as we shall see in a moment, every other decorative element of the space refers to John Barton, so an inscription on the tomb itself was perhaps a little superfluous. The only hint to his identification on the monument is the object supporting his feet. No lion or animal supporter for this no-nonsense merchant, but a barrel, or a 'tun' as it would have been known in the 15th century. Across the base of the tun is a bar, thus creating a punning rebus for his name: *Bar-tun*.

This extraordinary tomb

Figure 4 The cadaver effigy of John Barton. (Photo by Allan Barton)

Figure 5 A view looking onto the Barton chapel from the chancel, showing the tomb of Barton, the seating and the parclose screens. (Photo by Allan Barton.)

forms the centrepiece of an elaborate multi-media decorative scheme that stretched across the whole interior of the chapel of Our Lady and into the chancel, and extends outwards to the exterior of the building too.

The glazing of the chapel of Our Lady was an important element of this visual scheme. It survives in a very fragmentary condition, but enough remains, and there is sufficient evidence in antiquarian sources to piece it together and get some sense of what was once there and how it functioned visually. The iconographic scheme chosen for the three enormous four-light windows was a common typological series. The main lights of the windows were filled with large figures of the Apostles, each accompanied by scrolls with clauses from the Apostles' Creed. Very little remains of these except for elements of the scrolls and bits and bobs like the hat and cockleshell of St James the Great. Above the Apostles in the tracery lights were figures of Old Testament prophets, each neatly labelled. Of these the figures of Isaiah and Amos remain.

The iconography is fairly unremarkable, evidence of the patron's orthodox catholic faith, but what is remarkable about this glazing scheme is just how much evidence it contained of Barton's patronage. We know from the herald and antiquary Elias Ashmole, who visited the church on 28 August 1662, that the east window of the chapel, above the altar of Our Lady, incorporated donor images of John Barton and his family.[11] Barton was shown kneeling in a scarlet gown with his wife and their four sons and three daughters. The heads of two of the daughters are all that now remain. There were scrolls rising from their mouths with the rhyming Latin inscription 'Pater implora pro nobis mortis ut hora' – the figures were imploring God the Father for the salvation of their souls at the hour of

Figure 6 Fragments of glass removed from the windows of the chapel. From left to right: John Barton's merchant's mark, his initials and the Barton rebus. Below part of the memorial inscription from the east window of the chapel. (Photo by Allan Barton.)

death. One of these scrolls remains. Then above the donor figures, and presumably below the Apostles, was an inscription that invoked prayers for Barton, who it stated was both a merchant and sometime mayor of the Staple of Calais. Part of that inscription remains. Unifying the whole glazing scheme across all three windows were quarries, the diamond-shaped glazing elements behind the figures of the Apostles. These were powdered with various devices alluding to John Barton directly. In yellow stain were his initials J B repeated time and time again, and also his merchant's mark, the family firm's trademark applied to all his woolsacks on export to the continent. The Barton rebus, the tun with the bar, also makes an appearance. Lots of these devices still remain, and there would be more, had not a 19th-century evangelical vicar taken exception to the beer barrels in his church window and had many of them removed.[12] There was therefore no need for a memorial inscription on the tomb, for the window beside it and the whole glazing scheme in the chapel functioned together – the tomb and the glass were a single unified memorial to John Barton.

The altar of Our Lady was set below the window containing Barton's donor image, so the priest celebrating mass had a ready visual aid when it came to the commemoration of the departed that formed part the canon of the mass. The window and altar were framed on either side by two 8 ft tall canopied niches, which seemingly contained a tableau of the Annunciation. The near life-size image of Our Lady is still in situ. The chapel continued to be adorned by Barton's successors. His grandson, also called John Barton, gave up his estates in 1515 to become an observant friar, bequeathing in his will 'a table of Alabastre'

Figure 7 A panel of fragments, including remains of figures of Apostles. The curving scroll is all that remains of the donor image of John Barton. (Photo by Allan Barton.)

Figure 8 Glass from the windows of the Barton chapel and a Barton armorial from the north chancel windows. (Photo by Gordon Plumb.)

to the chapel of Our Lady[13] – a painted Nottingham alabaster altarpiece, perhaps like the Joys of the Virgin altarpiece now in the Victoria and Albert Museum.[14] Sadly the church roofs were all replaced in the 17th century, but the corbels still remain and they continue the theme embellished with the arms of the Staple of Calais and Barton's merchant's mark. It is probable, given the richness of the rest of the decorative scheme, that the lost flat ceilings would have been richly painted and may well have contained further evidence of Barton's patronage.

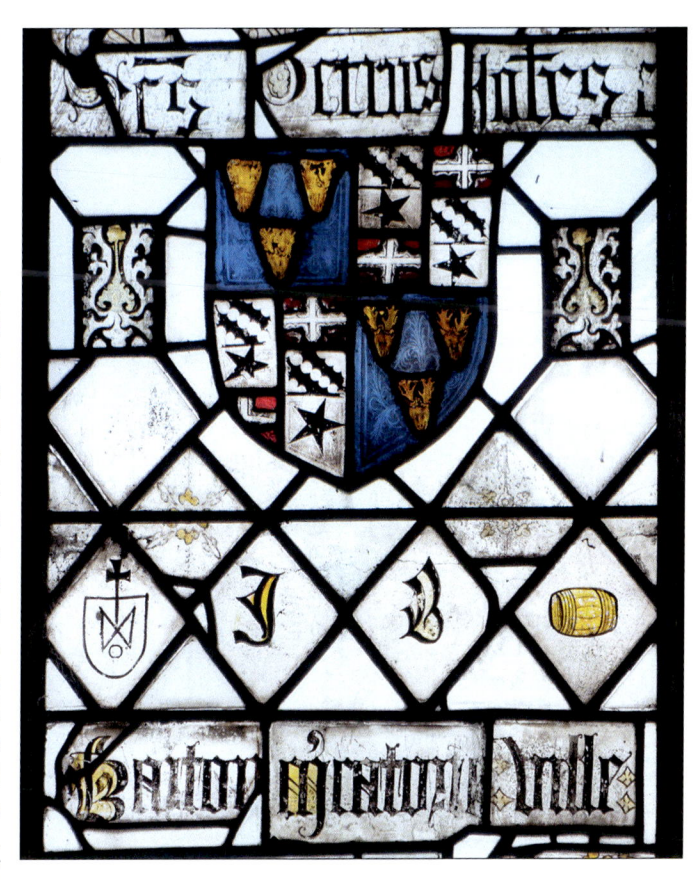

The stalls in the chapel are still in place. They are arranged in a semi-collegiate fashion, with returned stalls to the west and a rank of stalls facing north towards the chancel. Though rather battered now, these stalls were once extremely fine, and their bench-ends are still decorated with birds, animals and angels amid foliage. The stalls are almost certainly in their original position and were perhaps used by the Barton family during mass. Those occupying the chapel during the parish mass at the high altar would see the Elevation of the Host appearing above John Barton's tomb.

At one time all this Barton branding continued into the chancel,

Figure 9 The donor heads of John Barton's daughters. (Photo by Allan Barton.)

where the north windows, which can be viewed from the Our Lady's chapel through John Barton's tomb, were once filled with the same quarries as in the chapel and the Barton family arms.[15] Sadly these have now gone. Although it has now only a shadow of its late medieval splendour and is denuded of some of its decorative elements, even now John Barton's presence dominates every aspect of the church interior.

When we pass outside and examine the exterior, there is further evidence of Barton's patronage. The label stops of the west window and the buttresses of the tower are decorated with the Barton merchant's mark and the arms of the Staple of Calais.

However it is over the south porch that we find the most self-conscious example of personal expression and display. The porch at Holme was completed after John's death by his son Ralph, as a consequence of a provision made directly in his father's will, and Ralph appears to seamlessly continue the decorative scheme.[16] This two-storey structure originally towered over the shallow roofline of the south nave aisle. Approached by a path that slopes up to it, the porch though small, is a dramatic feature of the structure, and Ralph used that to great visual effect. Over the south doorway he incorporated a series of armorial panels that were intended to demonstrate not only his father's prestige, but also just how well connected and upwardly mobile the Barton family were becoming by the time of his father's death.

At the centre of the frieze are the arms of John Barton, the arms of the Staple of Calais, a shield charged with his merchant's mark and a couple of woolsacks, and one with the arms of Barton impaling Bingham, for John and his wife Isabella. Three of these shields are flanked by John's initials, and below one shield is another pun on the family surname, this time a bear holding a tun. Among the arms that appear here are those of John Stanhope impaling those of his wife Catherine Molyneaux. Of a similar age to Barton, Stanhope was a member of a long-established Nottinghamshire gentry family. He was a close associate of Barton and was made supervisor of his will.[17] Stanhope was also well connected socially and politically. He was an esquire of the chamber to King Henry VI and was also an MP for and sheriff of Nottinghamshire.[18] It was clearly through Stanhope's influence that the Barton family fortunes advanced, and that seems to be the motive for his inclusion here.

Stanhope's wife Catherine was a member of a prominent Lancashire family, the Molyneaux of Sefton. When she married Stanhope she was the widow of Ralph Radcliffe of Smithills Hall in Lancashire. Her daughter Joanna Radcliffe, Stanhope's stepdaughter, married Ralph Barton, John Barton's eldest son.[19] The arms of Ralph Barton above the porch illustrate that connection: they show Barton impaling Radcliffe, Walton and Norley.[20] Ralph's eldest son, named John like his grandfather, further solidified the connec-

Figure 10 The armorial panel over the entrance to the porch, a series of shields of arms of the Barton family and their associates. (Photo by Gordon Plumb.)

tion with the Radcliffe family, by marrying in 1486 his cousin Cecilia Radcliffe. Cecilia was the heiress to Smithills Hall and of extensive Lancashire property. As a consequence of that alliance, when this second John passed his estates to his son Andrew in 1515, Andrew was already established among the major landowners of Lancashire.[21]

What these panels over the porch demonstrate vividly is that John Barton's business acumen as a wool merchant bought not only a landed estate, but also good social connections for his family. The sheep paid not only for the material possessions that John enjoyed in his lifetime, but also for a rise in the social status of his descendants and ultimately the gentrification of his family.

Of course John Barton's work at Holme by Newark cannot be considered in isolation. Many of the merchant class were spending their newly found wealth on church building in the late 15th and early 16th centuries, and were similarly incorporating into that work evidence of their munificence. There is no space here for an exhaustive list of examples, but it is worth highlighting one or two that are more or less contemporary with Barton's work. Not far from Holme at Great Ponton near Grantham in Lincolnshire, Anthony Ellys, another Staple merchant built both a house and a new tower for the parish church. Like the porch and chapel at Holme, the tower was ludicrously out of scale with the rest of the church building – and incorporated decorative panels with both Ellys's arms and a little motto that echoes the one Barton uses in his house: 'thinke and thanke God of all'.[22] Like Barton, Ellys was enabled by his new-found wealth to establish a gentry dynasty.

In 1517 at Tiverton in Devon, a Merchant Adventurer, John Greenway, added to his parish church both a new south porch and a chantry chapel for himself. The work resembles that at Holme, but it rather leaves John Barton's decorative scheme looking spare and modest. At Tiverton the architecture is entirely subordinated to the decoration, as Greenway overlaid the new work with merchant's marks, his initials, coats of arms, Tudor roses and even images of his ships. Inside the porch over the main door and echoing the images in glass of John Barton, are kneeling donor images of Greenway and his wife, invoking the intercession of the Blessed Virgin Mary.[23]

The use of the family trade mark by merchants as a form of quasi-heraldry was common in the late Middle Ages, and occurred in many contexts, in both urban and rural locations. There are a number of Norwich examples. The 16th-century Renaissance terracotta tomb of Robert Jannys at St George's Colegate incorporates his merchant's mark. Jannys was a grocer who rose to the top of civic life in Norwich, serving two terms as mayor. He does not appear to be have been entitled to a coat of arms, and used his mark in lieu of a heraldic achievement. In the centre of his tomb his mark and his initials impale the arms of his wife on a shield.[24]

Another example is the early 16th-century Westgate pall from St Gregory's in Norwich, now in the Castle Museum. This is a covering of cloth of gold, used communally in the parish to cover the coffin at funerals. The only decoration on this rich cloth is a single roundel (originally one of four on the sides and ends of the pall), containing the merchant's mark of John Westgate, the donor, and the inscription 'Pray for the soul of John Westgate and Mawde his Wyff'. At every funeral in which this cloth was used, the congregation would be reminded of John and Maud.

What were John Barton and other members of his social class trying to achieve through the church building work they commissioned and its decoration? Was all this apparent

Figure 11 The Greenway porch and aisle at Tiverton in Devon, covered in emblems relating to the donor John Greenway. (Photo by Allan Barton.)

Figure 12 The surviving roundel from the Westgate pall, with the merchant's mark of John Westgate and an inscription asking for prayers for the soul of Westgate and his wife Maud. (Photo by Allan Barton.)

display of status, simply self-expression and self-aggrandisement? Certainly the work at Holme is self-conscious, and there is a clear sense that the work exists to some extent to mark John Barton's social achievements. However, behind that self-consciousness is a very clear spiritual motive. Erecting his transi tomb before his death is good evidence that John Barton was spiritually motivated and was thinking beyond this life to the next. The Apostles' creed, the images of the prophets in glass, the inscriptions incorporated into the fabric of his own home, are all evidence that God and the catholic faith were central to Barton's self-understanding, and that he saw his good fortune as God-given. Barton was a man who took his faith and his salvation seriously. On his tomb, we have the quote from Job, imploring us to have pity on Barton's soul. In glass, there was John Barton imploring for his own soul himself, directly. All around us are reminders of him and his family. The church of St Giles Holme is a record of his financial and social success, but it is equally a repository of memory. It is an interactive space, and John Barton intended all who saw it to interact with it. When Barton set about the rebuilding of this church, above all he was intent on creating, for want of a better word, an intercessory 'machine'. The purpose of all this personal display was ultimately to create a means by which perpetual prayers could be invoked for the good of his soul.

Acknowledgement

This paper is largely based on two theses: A. B. Barton, 'St Giles, Holme-by-Newark, Nottinghamshire: an analysis and contextualisation of a late fifteenth-century parochial chapel', unpublished MA dissertation, University of York, 1999; and A. B. Barton, 'The stained glass of Derbyshire and Nottinghamshire 1400–1550', unpublished PhD thesis, University of York, 2004, pp. 269–86.

Allan Barton *was awarded a PhD in History of Art at the University of York for a thesis focusing on the medieval stained glass of Nottinghamshire and Derbyshire. He is currently Chaplain to the University of Wales Trinity St David in Lampeter.*

Notes

1. E. G. Wake, *The History of Collingham and its Neighbourhood* (Newark, 1867), pp. 90–1; and N. Truman, *Holme by Newark Church and Its Founder* (Gloucester, 1946), p. 10.
2. *Calendar of Patent Rolls, Henry VI* (London, 1910), 6: pp. 211–12.
3. London, British Library, Harley MS. 1400, f. 69v.
4. *Calendar of Patent Rolls, Edward IV–Henry VI* (London, 1900), pp. 315–16.
5. York, Borthwick Institute for Archives, Episcopal Register 23, f.345r.
6. York, Borthwick Institute for Archives, Episcopal Register 23, ff. 345v-345r.
7. Thoroton, *The Antiquities of Nottinghamshire* (London, 1677), p. 349. The house was demolished in the second half of the 19th century. According to 19th-century sources, the inscription was repeated in the stonework of the house too, which was also elaborated with the Barton arms and fleur de lys. E. G. Wake, *The History of Collingham and Its Neighbourhood, Including the Northern Half of the Hundred of Newark* (Newark, 1867), p. 86; T. M. Blagg, 'Second excursion: the district around Collingham', *Transactions of the Thoroton Society*, 9 (1905), p. 35.
8. London, Public Record Office. E150/743, no. 13.
9. York, Borthwick Institute for Archives, Episcopal Register 23, f.345r.

10 York, Borthwick Institute for Archives, Episcopal Register 23, f.345r.
11 Oxford, Bodleian Library, Ashmole MS 854, pp. 144–5.
12 Based on a comment related to Nevil Truman while the glass was being conserved in 1933. Nottingham, Nottingham Archives Office, M 13923, f. 10v.
13 London, Public Record Office. E150/743, no. 13.
14 For this altarpiece see F. Cheetham, *English Medieval Alabasters: With a Catalogue of the Collection in the Victoria and Albert Museum* (Oxford, 1984), pp. 70–1.
15 Illustrated in a black and white engraving looking across the tomb of John Barton to the chancel beyond. W. D. Rastall, *A History of the Antiquities of the Town and Church of Southwell in the county of Nottingham* (London, 1787), plate bound in, no pagination or plate numbering.
16 York, Borthwick Institute for Archives, Episcopal Register 23, f.345r.
17 York, Borthwick Institute for Archives, Episcopal Register 23, f.345r.
18 S. Payling, *Political Society in Lancastrian England: The Greater Gentry of Nottinghamshire* (Oxford, 1991), pp. 114 and 148. *Calendar of Patent Rolls Preserved in the Public Record Office, Edward IV, Edward V, Richard III* (London, 1901), pp. 393–5, 397.
19 W. Langton (ed.), *The Visitation of Lancashire and part of Cheshire made in the Twenty Fourth Year of the Reign of King Henry the Eight A. D. 1533 by Special Commission of Thomas Benalt, Clarencieux,* Cheetham Society, vol. 110, part 2, pp. 198.
20 Langton, p. 197.
21 Langton, pp. 198 and 200.
22 N. Pevsner, J. Harris and N. Antram, *The Buildings of England: Lincolnshire* (London, 1989), pp. 332–3.
23 L. Stone, *Sculpture in Britain in the Middle Ages* (London, 1955), p. 223; A. Clifton-Taylor, *English Parish Churches Are Works of Art* (London, 1974), p. 120.
24 www.norwich-churches.org/monuments/Robert%20Jannys/Robert_Jannys.shtm) (accessed 5 March 2016).

Valuations of churches in medieval Norfolk

Elizabeth Gemmill

This paper introduces, in the context of the medieval county of Norfolk, a source which has been little used hitherto as an index of the wealth of the medieval Church: the inquisitions post mortem (IPMs) of the 13th and 14th centuries. The evidence presented has been garnered as part of an ongoing research project studying the valuations of ecclesiastical property in England and Wales made on the orders of royal government between the 13th and 15th centuries.

IPMs date from 1236 to c. 1640. They were royal inquiries made into the real property of tenants in chief of the Crown, usually after death but occasionally in other circumstances, such as the incapacity of the tenant to manage his own property, or exceptionally, forfeiture of the estates for felony or treason. The inquisitions were not always made immediately after the tenant's demise, but returns were often made with surprising speed. They were usually initiated by a writ issued from the king's chancery to the escheator, that is, the officer responsible for administering royal wardships. By far the majority of IPMs were initiated by the writ *diem clausit extremum* which ordered the escheator to take the lands of the deceased person into the king's hand, to keep them safely and to arrange for an inquisition into the extent and value of the lands. The writ used to initiate the process might vary depending on circumstance – for example, if the estates belonged to a deceased tenant in chief whose lands were in royal custody, or if the estates had been occupied by someone other than the king himself since the tenant's death. There were, from 1236, two main escheators, north and south of Trent, with subescheators working under them at county level. Apart from a brief period in Edward I's early years with using sheriffs as escheators, this was the arrangement until 1323, when a larger number of main escheatries was introduced. There were further adjustments to the arrangements in the early years of Edward III, but after 1341 the escheatries settled down to correspond to the shrievalties.[1]

Jurors, nearly always 12, were empanelled from the locality and sworn to answer the articles specified in the writ. Of the inquisitions conducted in relation to estates in Norfolk, many were held at Norwich, but they were held elsewhere too, sometimes on the individual manor under investigation. The resultant inquisition, sealed with seals of the 12 and the escheator's own seal (symbolizing their collective and shared responsibility), was returned to the chancery along with the writ to which it formed the response. Copies of the returns were kept in the chancery and were made for the royal exchequer – the latter to use as a reference when the escheator had to account for the issues arising from the custody of the estates. The fact that there is sometimes an extant exchequer copy of the inquisition gives the reader an additional source to check which is useful as many chancery IPM returns are in poor condition.

Some parts of country are better represented than others in the surviving returns. Broadly speaking, the south, the Midlands and the east are better represented than the north and the west. There is comparatively little for Wales.[2] This pattern is naturally replicated in the amount of information about churches. Thus, there is much more

All Saints, one of three medieval churches in the small village of Shotesham, and functioning today as the parish church (see page 79). Photo courtesy of James Gemmill.

evidence for churches in East Anglia than in Cheshire, Cornwall or Lancashire, but it is also the case that there were many more for parish churches in East Anglia than for those in some other parts of the country.

As well as patterns of survival of inquisitions and distribution of settlement, the amount of evidence about churches and other ecclesiastical institutions depends on the presence in the region of tenants in chief of the Crown whose death prompted inquiry. If a particularly important tenant in chief died, an especially thorough investigation might be conducted, perhaps involving supplementary inquiries. Of particular importance in the context of ecclesiastical interests was the use by chancery clerks of a form of the writ *certiorari* which asked the escheator to inquire into the true value of knight's fees and advowsons of churches. Requests initiated by this writ are encountered in particular in respect of the estates of larger tenants. That such writs specified the advowson of churches as well as fees is not clear from the calendars, which abbreviate the reference to the writ as '*certiorari de feodis*, etc.'

Knight's fees and advowsons were entirely different things, fees being the holdings by knight's service by the tenant in chief's own vassals, and advowsons of churches being the right to present clerks to ecclesiastical benefices and to exercise patronage rights in religious houses. Yet they were perhaps thought of in association with each other because the benefits fell in only periodically: the assets themselves were in the hands of others than the individual who was the subject of the inquisition. The *certiorari* writ focused attention on these two elements – fees and advowsons – and consequently elicited more information about them than did the standard *diem clausit extremum* writ. Moreover, the writs produced valuations of churches which responses to *diem clausit extremum* often omitted to include. Conversely, the information about advowsons tended to be given as a list, without details of the relationship between the advowson and the manor or other holding to which it may have belonged – information which did tend to be forthcoming in response to the *diem clausit extremum* writ. Responses to the *certiorari* writ, finally, often included a statement that the tenant had no fees or advowsons in the county, or none other than those which were listed in the return. Some responses to the writ also reported information about advowsons in the hands of the subject's own tenants

A writ was not only a series of instructions; it was the escheator's warrant for action. Many writs, when returned, were endorsed by the escheator with a memo of the action that he had taken, and the instructions in the writ itself might be replicated in the opening of the return, suggesting a strong 'audit trail' culture. The core questions in the *diem clausit extremum* writ were these: how much land the tenant had held of the king and how much of others, by what service, what it was worth, and the identity of the heir and his age. Later on a question was introduced about the date of the tenant's death. Conversely, early versions of the writ during the middle years of the 13th century itemized different sources of income and types of property – demesne lands, services, rents, villeinages and all issues of land, as well as knight's fees and advowsons of churches – but this level of detail was gradually abandoned, being superseded by the more summary version by the early years of Edward I's reign. As a guide to how he might proceed the escheator may have had recourse to other documents, such as the 'articles of the escheator' and 'how to make a manorial extent' – both of which date from the later 13th century.[3]

There has, in recent years, been a renaissance of interest in IPMs, resulting in a number of important scholarly achievements. In particular, they have been used as the key source for creating an atlas of lordship and of the exploitation of land and resources in the period up to the first outbreak of plague.[4] The calendaring of IPMs has now been completed up to 1447, so that there is now a continuous series from the earliest inquisitions of Henry III's reign up until that point. Progress is being made, through the Mapping the Medieval Countryside Project, towards making a freely available, searchable digital edition of the IPM calendars.[5] There is also a companion volume to the 15th-century inquisitions.[6] This recent work continues a long, though not unbroken, tradition of publication of IPMs, from the briefer Record Commission calendars to those published by HMSO from 1904 and the publication by county record societies of inquisitions relating to their own county.[7] The earlier calendars for the IPMs of the 13th and 14th centuries do not, however, include some of the valuable details which historians now treasure, such as the names of jurors or the manorial extents themselves. For the purpose of the present project, the fact that they do not publish the figures for the church valuations (although they do record the fact of the advowson of churches) means that the figures need to be obtained by consulting the manuscripts themselves.

Historians have called into question the reliability of valuations found in IPMs. They have drawn attention to the forces that would tend to depress the figures. The family might influence the escheator to under-report the estimated income so as to protect the heir's assets during a period of royal custody, and indeed low figures would take the pressure off the escheator himself when he was administering the estates. Those hopeful of being granted a royal wardship – as a favour or in payment of a royal debt – also had an interest in the land being under-valued. Another line of argument is that those involved had no particular motive for accurate reporting, and that the jurors themselves (perhaps especially when reporting about estates with which they were unfamiliar) may have relied overly on the information supplied by the escheator – who may in turn have relied on the record of previous inquiries.[8] If the latter were indeed the case, we should expect to find 'fossilized' figures, which did not take account of, for example, falling land values and rents or changes in land use. There were differences of recording practice and varying degrees of conscientiousness among escheators. Other problems with using the various kinds of valuation to make comparisons between regions are that there were different standards in use in different parts of the country, and there are various terms of only local application.[9]

All the above can be shown, on the strength of the Norfolk evidence discussed here, to be far less relevant to the valuations of churches than to other valuations encountered in this source. First, valuations of churches were recorded as sums of money which did not vary across the country – although what did vary within and between regions was the physical size of the individual parish, and this is a point to be taken into consideration when it comes to assessing the potential of the evidence as a guide to regional patterns of settlement and prosperity.

The material amassed thus far includes over 160 valuations of churches in Norfolk from the period 1265 to 1377. Valuations of churches were made, not because the landowner whose lands were being investigated actually received income from the tithes, glebe lands and offerings which formed the spiritual endowment of the benefice, but because the patronage of ecclesiastical benefices – the right to present a clerk to a church – was a right that belonged to land and was inherited with it. So too were the rights which the founders of some religious houses and their successors exercised in those houses, such as giving licence to elect a new head of house, to consent to the election once made, to keep custody of the house during vacancies, and the entitlement to hospitality and spiritual services.[10]

For the king, information about the value of a church or religious house gave him an indication how the patronage might best be used during a period of wardship. The king needed to know, for example, which rights belonged to the patron of a particular religious house and the worth of the house as a guide to the status of the place and what he might expect to get in a period of custody. He needed to know the value of individual churches as a guide to what sort of clerk might be presented to it should it fall vacant. Clerks working in royal administration were rewarded with benefices not only as and when such benefices became available, but on the basis of the value of those benefices. And of course the ecclesiastical interests, just like the estates themselves, needed to be divided fairly between co-heirs if the estates had to be partitioned, and if dower were to be assigned to a widow.

For all these reasons, it was important that the information be complete and accurate. Moreover, the family had an interest in seeing that the advowson rights were exercised because such use affirmed their ownership of them. A royal presentation to an ecclesiastical benefice served as evidence that the advowson belonged to the estate in question. Bishops' registers recorded that a presentation was made as a consequence of wardship patronage. To take just one example, when Henry de Thorp was instituted in the church of Broom in the deanery of Brooke on 22 March 1308 at the presentation of Edward II, it was made clear that this was by reason of the custody of the land and of William, son and heir of the late Roger de Brom.[11] The family during royal wardship of estates sometimes informed the king of the need to present, and would have been able to inform him about under-valuing of advowson rights in the case of dower assignment or partition.

There is evidence that the returns were done conscientiously. Sometimes escheators (or jurors) supplied additional information that had not been asked for – noting, for example, that a church was not vacant or that the advowson was litigious; or providing the name of the current incumbent or details of the endowment of the church or chapel; or specifying the order in which different patrons were entitled to present if the right of advowson was exercised by turns.

In the inquisition held at Fincham on 29 April 1325 into the fees and advowsons of Robert de Scales, it was reported that the patronage of the churches of Islington and Clenchwarton belonged to the manor of Islington from time out of mind, and that they had never been separated. Robert held the patronage jointly with his wife, but they had the right of presenting alternately with Thomas de Ingalnesthorp.[12] In an undated inquisition in response to the writ *certiorari* of 20 March 1332 it was reported that the advowson of the church of St Mary of Hockwold of the inheritance of Robert de Scales, a minor in the king's custody, was now vacant and that it was the turn of the king to present.[13] Edward III in fact presented Nicholas de Fontibus to Hockwold on 10 September 1332 by reason of the custody of Robert de Scales's lands.[14]

In an inquisition of November 1370, in response to a writ asking specifically about the details of Frederick Cokeruill of Tilney's demise of his property and who had occupied it, it was reported that he had given the advowson of Tilney to William Bardolf without royal licence. Details were provided of subsequent presentations and institutions of clerks to the church.[15] For those who lived in the locality, such information would be well known, unless perhaps the advowson had been granted out since the most recent presentation. Indeed, the IPM evidence studied thus far has proven consistent with the evidence from other records with regard to the ownership of patronage rights.

The patronage (or advowson) of a church was often associated with lordship of a manor, but also with the settlement of the local community. The correlation between manor, parish and community settlement seems complete in the case of Hockering in an undated inquiry of 1282–3. It was reported that the advowson of the church of the vill belonged to John le Marescal's manor of Hockering.[16] But such correspondence was of course by no means always the case. It was possible for the advowson of two churches to belong to a single manor, as in a return of 7 October 1275 when the advowsons of Castle Rising and Wootton were said to belong to Robert de Monte Alto's manor of Castle Rising.[17] Sometimes the patronage of a church was divided between patrons, with the landowner under consideration presenting by turns; elsewhere the church itself might have been divided so that the patron had only a moiety of the benefice in his gift. And, of course, many lay patrons granted out their patronage of churches to religious institutions.

The responses of jurors and escheators sometimes suggests uncertainty about the significance of the value of patronage to the patron, when he himself was not entitled to receive the income of a church. Most often it was the annual value of the church itself which was given. In 1343 the advowson of 'Shepedene' of which John Brom was patron was said to be worth nothing per year in itself, but the church was said to be worth £4 13s 4d per year.[18] In an inquisition at Wells next the Sea on 23 November 1347 the advowson of the church of Wells was said to be worth nothing per year. No valuation of the church was made.[19] By contrast the church of Kettlestone was said in January 1374 to be worth 12 marks (£8) per year 'when it happens'.[20] In the latter instance the jurors seem to have been implying that the potential value for the patron was realized when the church was vacant, but in fact this return was in response to a *certiorari* writ and the knight's fees were similarly treated.

We are told very little about how the valuations were made, and it is very rare for any breakdown of the value to be provided. In an inquiry into the manors and advowsons held by Robert de Tony in January 1310, the church of Necton

St Mary, Shotesham, demonstrating the density of medieval churches in Norfolk. Although not the parish church, it still hosts services. Photo courtesy of James Gemmill.

with its vicarage was valued at £25 per year.[21] In the valuation of Tilney mentioned above, the church was said to be worth £80 per year over and above the cost of repairs. The figures are usually in round sums, or if shillings and pence are specified, the total value nearly always corresponds to an exact number of marks (one mark being 13s 4d). Sometimes we are told that a given church is worth a certain amount 'in normal years'. We may take from this that valuations were perhaps intended to be approximate rather than based on detailed investigations into the tithes or glebe lands. The question is therefore whether the valuations were made by those with local knowledge of the value of the church, or if the information was merely lifted from existing records.

One possibility is whether the information was taken from the readily available papal assessments of benefices made in the 13th century, and in particular the 'Valuation of Norwich' of 1254 (so called because it was made under the authority of Walter of Suffield, bishop of Norwich[22]) or the Taxatio of Nicholas IV 1291–2, which was the assessment for a papal tax of a tenth on ecclesiastical income for Edward I's intended crusade.[23] Since the latter was used as the basis for royal and papal taxation for the rest of the medieval period, it might be thought that escheators would use it.

A few valuations of East Anglian churches of the later 13th century were said to be based on the 1254 assessment. Although that assessment had covered the country as a whole, there seems to have been a special awareness of it in IPM returns in East Anglia because it had been made on the authority of the local bishop. Thus the church of Shotesham in 1287 was assessed at 10 marks according to the assessment of Walter, bishop of Norwich.[24] Bowthorpe in 1290 was estimated at 10 marks per year according to the estimation of Bishop Walter.[25] References to Bishop Walter and his assessment decline in the early 14th century but were not replaced by references to the Taxatio of 1291–2. And a comparison of a substantial sample of valuations in IPMs of the 14th and 15th centuries with those in the Taxatio shows that this was generally not the source. Moreover, churches and chapels whose value was too low to be included in papal valuations were included in IPMs. For example, in 1334 the church of St Margaret Waxham was said to be below the threshold for (tax) assessment but to be worth 40s per year;[26] the church was not included in the Taxatio.

Shotesham St Martin's, a ruin for centuries. Photo courtesy of James Gemmill.

Another source might have been the valuations made of the estates in previous IPMs. It would have been natural to consult copies kept locally of such returns if to do so were accepted as a way of proceeding. Yet comparisons of two IPMs taken on the estates of the earls of Norfolk in 1270 and 1307 show that this was not done routinely.[27] And indeed the evidence of a sample of Norfolk churches occurring in successive inquisitions over the 13th and 14th centuries shows that escheators were able to note a change in the value of churches.

Where we have two or more valuations spread over the period there is evidence of a significant drop in value for most, 25–33 per cent being typical. In some instances, the loss of value appears to have begun before the Black Death of 1348–9.[28] No reason is given in the returns for these changes, although there is occasionally evidence from elsewhere showing an awareness of loss of value. For example, in the inquisition on the estates of Andrew Harclay, earl of Carlisle, in 1323, half of the advowson of the churches of Sedburgh and Dent was reported to have been worth (*solebat valere*), with glebe, 100 marks per year, but was now (*modo*) worth 60 marks.[29] Given the location of the estates it seems likely that this was a result of the Anglo-Scottish war. In no part of the country, however, have explicit statements yet been found in inquisitions to 1377 that there had been a decline in the worth of individual churches as a result of the Black Death – although post-1348 IPMs did report on other ways in which the pestilence had affected revenues and land use.

There was enormous variety between the values of individual churches – from Swaffham at £80 in 1280 to St Margaret Waxham at 40s as shown above.[30] The value of churches within the patronage of individual patrons was also hugely variable. So, for example, in an inquisition in response to the writ *certiorari* on the fees and advowsons of Robert Morle made in 1362, the church of Hengham was worth 50 marks per year, Brandon 10 marks, 6s 8d, Little Burgh about 73s (the pence are not legible), a moiety of North Tuddenham £8, Foulsham £30, and Bintree 20 marks.[31]

This variability is confirmed by reference to the churches in the gift of Mary, countess of Norfolk (second wife of Thomas of Brotherton, earl of Norfolk) who died in about 1361.[32] The inquiry of 1362 made in response to a *certiorari* writ included a number of Norfolk churches of small value. The lowest in value was Antingham at 5 marks; the average mean value of the seven churches was just over 12½ marks.[33] It was the overall number of the churches in a patron's gift that was the measure of his or her status, rather than the value of the individual churches. So members of the nobility tended to have a number of churches in their gift rather than patronage of particularly wealthy churches. In addition to her advowsons in Norfolk, the countess of Norfolk had the patronage of 12 churches in Suffolk and of one in Gloucestershire.[34]

Evidence for the medieval ecclesiastical history of Norfolk is remarkably rich. The landscape – urban and rural – is everywhere articulated with parish churches and the material evidence is complemented by an array of written records – the Norfolk Domesday, the Acta of individual bishops, cartularies of religious houses, tax assessments of ecclesiastical institutions and, from 1299, the episcopal registers for the Norwich diocese.[35] Taken together with these, the evidence of the IPMs offers an exciting opportunity not only to study the medieval Church itself – the distribution and control of patronage and the careers of individual clergy – but also to examine regional and local patterns of settlement and prosperity, and to perceive how these may have changed over time during this crucial period.

Elizabeth Gemmill *is an associate professor in history at the University of Oxford and a fellow of Kellogg College. Her research interests are in medieval valuations of property, prices of consumables, and ecclesiastical patronage.*

Notes

1   See Christine Carpenter's 'General introduction to the New Series' in *Calendar of Inquisitions Post Mortem,* Vol. XXII 1–5 Henry VI (142–7) ed. Kate Parkin (London and Woodbridge: TNA and Boydell Press, 2003), pp. 2–9. The changes are summarized in Bruce Campbell and Ken Bartley, *England on the Eve of the Black Death: An Atlas of Lay Lordship, Land and Wealth, 1300–1349* (Manchester University Press, 2006), p. 18. For a brief introduction to the office of the escheator and its historiography thus far, see 'The escheator: a short introduction' in

the 'Mapping the medieval countryside: property, places and people', www.inquisitionspostmortem.ac.uk/contexts/the-escheator-a-short-introduction/ (accessed 13 January 2016).
2 Campbell and Bartley, *England on the Eve of the Black Death*, pp. 29–34.
3 See Elizabeth Gemmill, *The Nobility and Ecclesiastical Patronage in Thirteenth-Century England* (Woodbridge: Boydell Press, 2013), pp. 115–16 and references there cited.
4 Campbell and Bartley, *England on the Eve of the Black Death*.
5 See www.winchester.ac.uk/academicdepartments/history/research/inquisitions/Pages/TheInquisitionsPost-MortemProject.aspx and http://www.inquisitionspostmortem.ac.uk/ for details of the project.
6 Michael Hicks (ed.), *The Fifteenth-Century Inquisitions Post Mortem: A Companion* (Woodbridge: Boydell Press, 2012).
7 See Carpenter, 'General introduction', pp. 1–2 and notes.
8 See Gemmill, *Nobility and Ecclesiastical Patronage*, p. 114 and references.
9 Campbell and Bartley, *England on the Eve of the Black Death*, esp. pp. 35–40.
10 See Gemmill, *Nobility and Ecclesiastical Patronage*, pp. 3–4 for a brief summary of the historiography of monastic patronage in England.
11 Norwich Record Office, DN, Reg 1/1 (Register of John Salmon), f. 27r.
12 TNA C134/89(21), m6 (*CIPM*, VI. p.371 no 593.
13 TNA C135/33(8), m2 (*CIPM*, VII. p. 338, no 476).
14 *CPR 1330–1334*, p. 327.
15 TNA C135/215(16), m.2 (*CIPM*, XIII. p. 14 no. 16).
16 TNA C 133/34(8), m. 5 (*CIPM*, II. p. 281 no. 471).
17 TNA C 133/10(6), m6 (*CIPM*, II. p. 84 no. 128).
18 TNA C 135/68(3), m2 (*CIPM*, VIII.p.279, no. 412).
19 TNA C 135/87, m.26 (*CIPM*, IX. p. 59 no. 56).
20 TNA C135226, m.44 (*CIPM*, XIII. p. 137, no. 167).
21 TNA C 134/15(3), m.12 (*CIPM*, V. p. 102, no. 198).
22 W. E. Lunt, *The Valuation of Norwich* (Oxford: Clarendon Press, 1926).
23 *Taxatio Ecclesiastica Angliae et Walliae Auctoritate P. Nicholai IV, c. 1291* ed. T. Astle, S. Ayscough and J. Caley (Record Commission, 1802). The Taxatio is now available as an online database hosted by the Humanities Research Institute at the University of Sheffield: www.hrionline.ac.uk/taxatio
24 TNA C 133/49 (15), m.7 (*CIPM*, II. p. 404, no. 653). The church of St Mary, Shotesham was valued at 10 marks in the 1254 valuation: Lunt, *Valuation of Norwich*, p. 400.
25 The church of Bowthorpe was, however, valued at 5 marks in the valuation of 1254: Lunt, *Valuation of Norwich*, p. 398.
26 C 135/74(8), m.9 (*CIPM*, VIII. p. 375, no. 529).
27 Gemmill, *Nobility and Ecclesiastical Patronage*, p. 122.
28 Banningham was worth 20 marks in 1270, 16 marks in 1307 and 15 marks in 1362 (TNA C 132/38 (17), m.14, C133/127, m.30, C 135/173(1), m.10; Bintree 30 marks in 1282 and 20 marks in 1362 (C 133(34)8, m.9 and C 135/171(26), m.2); Brandon 10½ marks in 1316 and in 1362 (C 134/57(3), m.8 and C 135/171(26), m.2); Brockdish 40 marks in 1307 and 13 marks in 1362 (C133/127, m.30 and C 135/173(1), m.10); Bixley 24 marks in 1307 and 100s in 1362 (C 133/127, m.30 and C 135/173(1), m.10); Clenchwarton 15 marks in 1283 and £10 in 1325 (C 133/34(9), m.2 and C 134/89(21), m.6); Ellingham 24 marks in 1307 and 10 marks in 1362 (C 133/127, m.30 and C 135/173(1), m.10); Foulsham 60 marks in 1282, 40 marks in 1316 and £30 in 1362 (C 133/34(8), m.9, C 134/57(3), m.8 and C 135/171(26), m.2); Little Fransham 20 marks in 1264 and £10 in 1310 (C 132/31(3), m.4 and C 134(15)3, m.12); Hengham 80 marks in 1283 and 50 marks in 1362 (C 133/34(8),

m.10 and C 135/171(26), m.2); Necton 30 marks in 1264 and £25 in 1310 (C 132/31(3), m.4 and C 134/15(3),m.12); North Tuddenham (moiety) 20 marks in 1282, 11 marks in 1316 and £8 in 1362 (C 133/34(8), m.5, C 134/57(3), m.8 and C 135/171(26), m.2); Weeting St Mary £10 in 1303 and 1327 (C 133/106(20), m.7 and C 135/3(4), m.8).

29   TNA C134/74(14),m.2(*CIPM*, VI. p. 222, no. 378).
30   C 133/26(6)m5r; E 36/69f12v (*CIPM*, II. p. 212, no. 381)
31   TNA C 135/171 (26), m. 2 (*CIPM*, XI. p. 282, no. 365). The number of pence in the valuation of Bergh Parua is illegible.
32   Scott L. Waugh, 'Thomas , first earl of Norfolk (1300–1338)', *Oxford Dictionary of National Biography*, Oxford University Press, 2004, http://ezproxy-prd.bodleian.ox.ac.uk:2167/view/article/27196, accessed 12 January 2016.
33   The churches were South Walsham (28 marks), Banningham (15 marks), Stockton (10 marks), Ellingham (10 marks), Brockdish (13 marks), Bixley (100s) and Antingham. TNA C 135/173(1), m.10 (*CIPM*, XI. p. 310, no. 397).
34   TNA C 135/173(1), mm.10, 11 and 13 (*CIPM*, XI. p. 310, no. 397).
35   Norwich Record Office, DN Reg/1/1: Register of John Salmon, 1299–1325. For evidence of the existence of earlier registers of the diocese which have not survived, see David M. Smith, *Guide to Bishops' Registers of England and Wales: A Survey from the Middle Ages to the Abolition of Episcopacy in 1646* (London: Royal Historical Society, 1981), p. 150. John Salmon's register is being edited by the present author for the Canterbury and York Society.

The funeral of John Paston

Susan Curran

Let me start with a list (Table 1): a note of costs the Paston family paid out that were broadly related to John Paston's funeral, which took place in late May and early June of 1466. This list was printed in the 1904 edition of the *Paston Letters and Papers*, with the details taken from Blomefield's *History of Norwich*, although the original list that Blomefield worked from had by then been lost. I have modernized the spelling but not otherwise edited it. We shall come back to it later, and all you need to do now is to take in that it's a very long list. And it should be apparent even from a quick skim that it provides us with details of a very elaborate and expensive set of rituals related to John Paston's death.

One of the problems in working with the Paston letters is that this wonderful resource is to a large extent unique. There's no comparable set of papers surviving from any other provincial gentry family of their era, and to the best of my knowledge there are no comparable notes of funeral expenses for other individuals in John Paston's class. And of course medieval funerals were not very much like modern funerals. So it is a very tricky business to try to judge how the funeral of John Paston compares with other people's funerals, simply because I don't know, and I'm not sure that anyone really does know, very much about the finer details of medieval funerals. We have glimpses of what they were like, but not a great deal more than that.

But I feel I can confidently say one thing from the evidence of this list: that John Paston's was a very, very lavish funeral. It's obvious that it was enormously more lavish than say a farm labourer's funeral would have been, but I think it's fairly clear that it was also pretty lavish by the standards of men of John Paston's own class. We do have some remarkable funerary monuments surviving from around this era, and it's a fair guess that the funerals of the people they commemorate were also grandiose affairs, so I am not suggesting that this funeral was as unique as the surviving record of it is. But all the same, I think it was pretty exceptional. This was a big, big funeral.

One measure of that, although it too is not a simple one for us to assess today, is the sheer cost of it. This is a bill of costs, so one obvious thing to do is to add them up. Some of these entries might be duplicates, and in other cases we can't be sure quite how the sums were done, but I have had a go, and I reckon the total comes to around £247. Of course, that's only a note of the cash the family paid out. It doesn't include the wages of the family's many regular staff, who would have put in a lot of time and effort over the funeral plans, and I'd guess there were quite a lot of contributions from other people that were not repaid in cash and also don't figure in the list. For instance, we know the Pastons used a length of cloth of gold, which was seriously expensive, to cover the coffin, but that doesn't figure in this list.

This list also gives us a sense of the typical wage for a working man at that time. It was around 4d a day. So if we assume the average man worked on average for 250 days a year (which is high by modern standards, and probably too high for that era too), we are looking here at around 60 years' income for a plain man being spent on this one funeral and the related costs.

Table 1 **John Paston's funeral expenses**

	£	s	d
Paid by James Gloys (the family chaplain) at Norwich when the corpse was there and before			
Four orders of friars that rode out to meet the corpse	8		
Alms		2	7
23 sisters of Norman's Hospital, Norwich, 4d each, and to their Warden, 8d		8	4
Offering on Pentecost Tuesday			1
The hearse		40	
24 yards of broad white cloth for gowns		27	8
Dyeing the cloth		4	
For setting on the tents			6
Another 22 yards and 3 quarters of broad white cloth		34	3
For 'grownedyng'		3	4
Dyeing		3	
38 priests at the dirge at Norwich when the corpse lay there		12	8
39 children with surplices within the church and without		4	4
26 clerks with 4 keepers of the torches, 2d each		3	4
Clerks of St Peter's [Hungate] and St Stephen's Norwich for the ringers at the arrival of the corpse		2	
Prioress of Carrow		6	8
and a maid that came with her			2
To the anchoress			40
In alms		15	
A woman that came from London with the corpse to Norwich		6	8
Paid by Richard Calle (business agent) and Gloys at Bromholm			
To the prior to meet the deceased's bequest		40	
Nine monks, 6s 8d each		3	
One other monk of the same place (Bromholm?)			20
Bringing the abbess with torches			20
To the prior's butler for bread		2	10

	£	s	d
Washing napery			12
To the butler for his reward			20
To the baker for 310 eggs			19
To him for his reward		3	4
To 28 beds with clothes and washing of the same		5	
Two men that filled the grave			8
Brewing of 5 corns of malt			20
9 pounds of candles			11
To the clerks of Bromholm			8
8 pieces of pewter of the prior's that were lost			20
Given among the men of the bakehouse to the parish church of Bromholm		10	
12 'schyrchys' (searchers?)		1	8
The priest that came with the corpse from London		3	4
Servitors who waited on him by commandment of William Paston (the deceased's brother)			21
To Playters for his offering			4
Vicar of Upton		2	
To the sexton of Bromholm for 22 crosses given to Marget and Modeley per John Paston		4	6
14 ringers		7	
24 servitors, 4d each		8	
70 servitors, 3d each		17	6
Paid to John Daubeney (a Paston servant) for more servitors		7	
Fish the day after the interment		6	10
Six barrels of beer		12	
A cask of red wine (15 gallons)		1	11
Hire of a horse for 3 days for Sir James (Gloys)			12
A quarter of malt		5	
4 bushels of wheat			32
A quarter of oats		2	8
10 combs of brewing malt			40
The board of Richard Harmer, 'wrythe' (wheelwright?), 3 days, and his hire for those days			32

	£	s	d
The board of William Young, barber, five days, and his hire for those days			16
Six pounds of candles			7
12 poor men bearing torches, six days from London to Norwich at 4d a day, and three days back home at 6d a day			309
Bread and ale for the torchbearers			13
To Martin Savage and Denschers waiting upon John Paston in London for seven days before he was carried thence		2	10
Bread bought		24	
7 barrels of beer		17	6
A barrel of the best quality		3	4
4 barrels of ale		13	4
Bread and ale for the 12 torchbearers			13
Alms to the poor at Bromholm	5	13	4
To William Collins, one of the butlers at Bromholm			12
To Wate Webster, another butler			12
To Gregory Worsteler, one of the porters at Bromholm			4
The parson at Mautby and Sir Thomas Lines, to the priests at the dirge at Bromholm		18	
In alms		47	5
and more alms		20	
To the glazier for taking out 2 panes of the church windows to let out the reek of the torches at the dirge and for soldering them back again			20
Victuals bought by Richard Charles			
27 geese		17	
27 'franked geese'		6	8
17 chickens		16	6
10 chickens			10
41 pigs		13	10
49 calves	4	13	4
34 lambs		27	2
22 sheep		37	5
10 neat [cattle]	4	16	1

THE FUNERAL OF JOHN PASTON

	£	s	d
2 'napronnes' to Richard Lynstede			10
Clarets and fawcetts			6
1300 eggs		6	6
20 gallons milk			20
8 gallons cream		2	8
4 pints of butter			4
1 quarter and 2 bushels of wheatmeal		7	10
To the parson of Crostweyt for a quarter of wheat		6	
13 gallons of ale		2	
To a labourer of 3 days			12
24 gallons of ale		4	
13 salt fish		4	4
For the purveying of bread, ale, and fish		3	4
To William Reynolds for lodging Master Prowet, Sir Thomas Lindes and another for two nights			6
For bread, ale and possets to the same persons			6
To Herman for flaying beasts for 3 days, 2s, and to John Foke for 3 days			20
For purveying of all the veal, lamb, beasts, certain pigs and poultry			40
Bill of the prior of Bromholm			
Memorandum: the prior took to board divers persons labouring about the interment, beginning the Thursday in Pentecost week			
On Thursday I find 3 persons who had 12d for their board and hire; on Friday 5 who had 15d; on Saturday 8 who had 13d. On Monday all were employed; and on the day after I find 4 to be allowed for their board 4d each, and for their hires 5d to 9d. Possibly this comes to:			71
Delivered by the prior to Richard Charles:			
first, 5 quarters of oats,		13	4
5 swine		12	6
1 bushel of 'mestlyn'			15
5 pounds of candles			5
20 quarters of malt		13	4
and with grinding and brewing		18	

	£	s	d
For a cartful of hay		4	4
For 2 swine		5	
For 2 bushels of oats			8
For a quarter of herring			6
For half a quarter of mackerel (each)			7
To the parson of St Peters for his fee of the wax about the cours, besides 2 candles of 1 lb and 1 half candle of a pound			20
At my master's 30th day for offering			1
Given to churches and in alms by James Gresham on the way to Bromholm 5 marks (1 mark = 13s 4d)	3	6	
To the clerk of St Peter Hungate and his fellowship when the corpse was in the church there			12
To Daubeney for beasts and other stuff for the interment	20		
To him in gold to change into small money for the dole	40		
To W. Peacock, in 3 bags to bear to Bromholm, in copper, the 20th day, 26 marks	17	6	8
To Madeley for his reward, 4 marks, and the same to Maryot	5	6	8
To Maryot for costs he bore on the way to Bromholm	3	12	
More to Madeley for money paid by him		41	10
To the keeper of the inn where John Paston died		20	
To Paston Church		10	
To Bacton Church		6	8
To Gresham the London carrier, in full payment for the Chandler of London	5	19	4
More in alms money		6	8
More for wine and beer, 7 marks	4	13	4
To the Parson of St Peters		6	8
Wine for the singers when the corpse was at Norwich		20	
To Skolehouse in part of his bill for torches and wax made at Bromholm to burn upon the grave, 4 marks	2	13	4
For 10 yards of narrow black for the Vicar of Dalling and Robert Gallawey, and for 3 yards and a quarter of broad cloth for Illee		2	10
To Fritton church		6	8
For a cope called a frogge of worsted for the Prior of Bromholm		26	8
For bread at the interment		9	

THE FUNERAL OF JOHN PASTON

	£	s	d
In alms		8	4
In wine and spices		1	
To Dom. John Loveday for cloth for a riding cope for himself		14	2
To the making of Reedham steeple		8	4
To John Orford, wax chandler, for 12 torches and 1 candle of 1 lb		15	2
To John Dewe for grey linen cloth and a silk fringe for the hearse	6	16	2
Given to the Austin friars at Yarmouth		75	
To Daubeney to keep the year-day at Bromholm the first year after his death	8	2	4
At Caister to 25 householders, 2d each		4	2
To the Master of the College at Caister		6	8
To Master Clement Felmingham at the same time		6	8
To eight priests at Caister at the same time		2	8
To children in surplices and other poor folk at the said time			14
To the paston of Hungate		6	8
To the said parson for a mass until Michaelmas next after the sayd year day		8	8
To Skolous, wax chandler, for making the hearse at Bromholm	22	9	8
To Philip Curson, draper, for cloths		9	3
To Aubrey, draper		34	
For a quarter of mackerel			12
To the prior of Bromholm for malt spent at the interment		40	
A light kept on the grave		10	
At Christmas next after the yearday to each of the four orders of friars, 10s each		40	
To the Vicar of Dalling for bringing home a pardon from Rome to pray for all our friends' souls		8	4
For a black gown to the said vicar		8	

Source: James Gairdner (ed.), *The Paston Letters* (1904), vol. IV, pp. 226–31 (taken from a lost document drawn on by Blomefield's *Norfolk*, vi. 483).

The society of the 1460s was not an egalitarian one, so this was not 60 years' income for John Paston, of course. We have a sense of his income from Roger Virgoe's analysis of a Norwich taxation list of 1451 (Table 2). As Virgoe pointed out, most people on the list probably understated their income, so we can only regard it as a fairly rough guide. The very richest person making a return (Lady Katherine Felbrigg) reported an income of £100 a year. Only 14 people in Norwich admitted to an income of over £20 a year, and one of them was John Paston, who declared £66, so he was among the richest handful of individuals in Norwich, one of the richest cities in England at the time. Agnes Paston, his mother, made the top 14 too, with about two-thirds as much income as her son. (Notice too that plenty of people who were reckoned liable to pay taxes earned a lot less than that working man's income I totted up very roughly just now. So that £66 means that the funeral expenses came to around four years' income for John Paston, but it was more like a hundred years' income for John Brewyn the baker or Richard Poringland the clerk.)

Could the Paston family afford that kind of payout, at the time when John Paston died? The short answer is no, for reasons I shall come on to shortly. And was John Paston the

Table 2 **A Norwich taxation list of 1451**

Isabella, Lady Morley	£82
John Wodehouse	£26
Lady Katherine Felbrigg	£100
John Ferrerys	£40
John Bacon	£33
Sir Henry Inglose	£66
Sir John Heveningham	£66
William Rokewood	£50
John Wyndam	£66
Agnes Paston	£40
Elizabeth Clere	£45
John Paston	£66
John Pagrave	£33
Thomas Gurnay	£50
...	
The Dean of St Mary in the Fields	£13
The Master of the Hospital of St Giles	£12
The Alderman of the Fraternity of St George	£4
John Gerard, 'bocher'	£2
John Thurton, 'candeler'	£2
John Buklee, cook	£6
John Brewyn, baker	£3
Richard Poryngland, clerk	£2

Source: selected entries from a list of income (from land and tenements) of taxpayers in Norwich, 1451, reproduced in Roger Virgoe, 'A Norwich taxation list of 1451', *Norfolk Archaeology*, **40**(2), pp. 145–54 (p. 149).

kind of major figure who really needed this kind of funeral? Frankly, the answer to that is no as well. Not only was he no aristocrat, he was not even a knight. (He had paid the fee that men who met the property qualification had to pay if they were not willing to take on knightly obligations.) He had not played a particularly prominent role in public life, and he had never fought for either of the rival kings whose supporters were then slugging their way through the Wars of the Roses. Nor was he the kind of much-loved figure whose funeral is guaranteed to draw a crowd of thousands out of sheer grief and affection. So one very interesting question is, why did the Pastons do this? What made them arrange such a massive funeral and spend so much on it?

I suggest some answers to that here. First I look briefly at exactly who John Paston was: at his family, his background and his life. I look at some of the issues that occupied his family at the time of his death, and what they might have wanted to achieve through the funeral. Then I dissect the list of expenses in some more detail, and look at what it tell us about the choices the Pastons made. And lastly, I look at the aftermath of the funeral, and some of the follow-up narrative that we can draw from the Paston papers.

The Paston family came to prominence with the generation before our John Paston. His father William was generally reckoned to have come from a family of bondmen: that is, serfs who had formal obligations to their landlord, and a limited right to own property. William was clearly an exceptional man, and with some help from his extended family he got a good education and became a lawyer, and later on a judge. He had a formidable career in public life, and he also made a fortune. It is fairly clear from the letters and papers that he achieved this by treading on a lot of other people, and as a result he was not universally popular.[1] He married quite late in life, to an heiress who brought property of her own to the marriage, so by the end of his life he had risen from obscurity to be one of the richest and most powerful men in East Anglia.

Our John Paston was his eldest son, and the task that he took on after his father's death was to consolidate the family's new position in the upper ranks of society. That was not an easy task. John Paston does not seem to have been nearly as exceptional a man as his father, and nor did he inherit all the property his father had effectively controlled. His mother not only outlived his father, she outlived him too, so she held on to that £40 a year throughout John Paston's life. And although he too married an heiress, his father's estate also had to make some provision for his brothers and his sister, so he did not get all the section of it that his mother did not hold on to.

One other real problem was that because the Pastons were not a well-established family, and John Paston was only in his early 20s when his father died, some people evidently thought that the judge's death would make them vulnerable. Not only might they have lost the social status the judge had established, they also faced challenges to their ownership of land. There were rival claims for example to Oxnead, which was Agnes Paston's home estate,[2] and Gresham, which had been given to John Paston and his wife on their marriage. It seems likely the Pastons had a valid title to these lands, but the claims caused them a great deal of difficulty, and indeed in early 1449 the Pastons were physically thrown out of Gresham, and a great deal of damage was done to their land and possessions, although they managed to reclaim the estate later.[3]

With threats like this facing him, it is not really surprising that John Paston learned

The Paston family

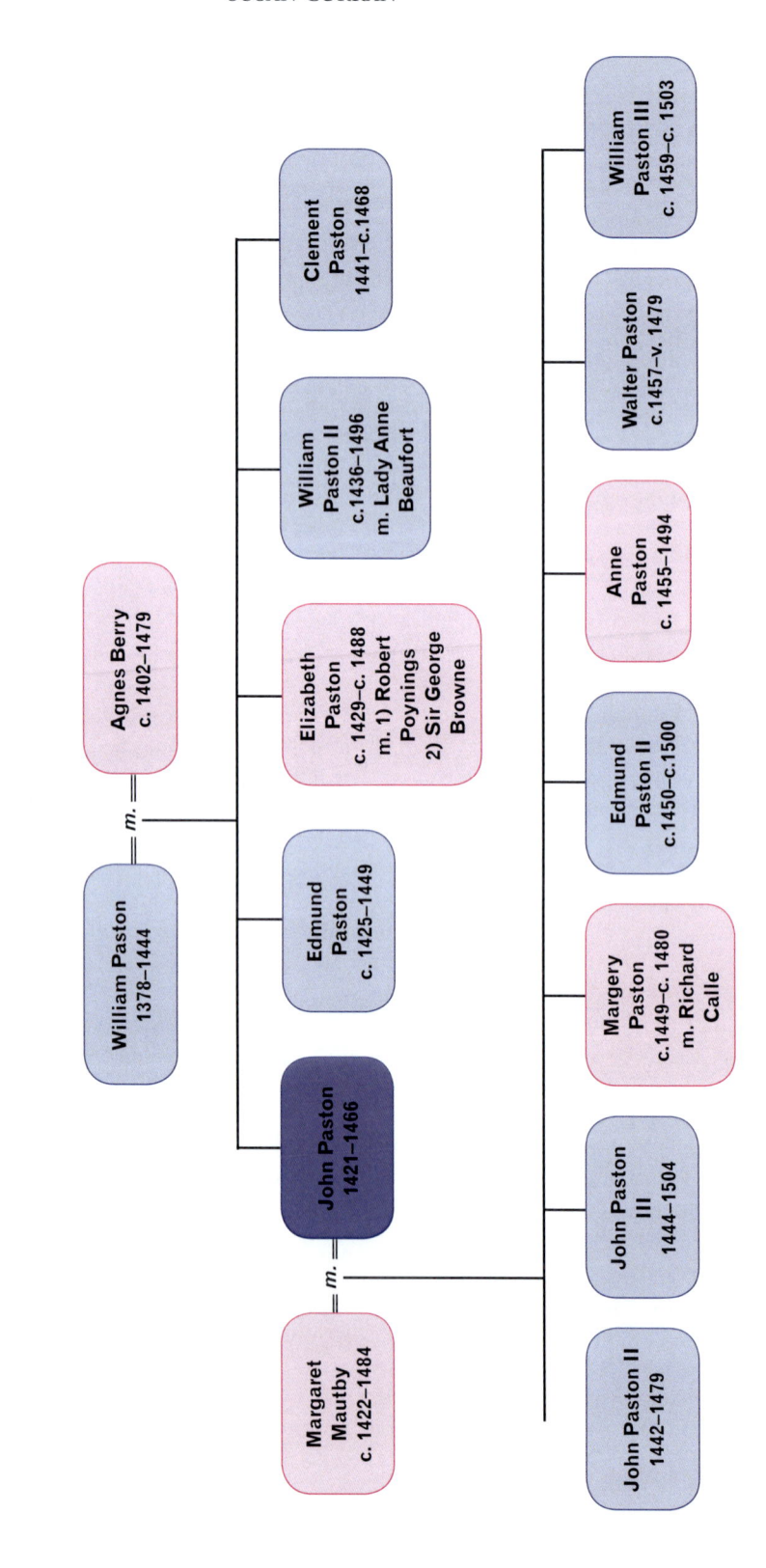

- **William Paston** 1378–1444 — m. — **Agnes Berry** c. 1402–1479
  - **Edmund Paston** c. 1425–1449
  - **John Paston** 1421–1466 — m. — **Margaret Mautby** c. 1422–1484
    - **John Paston II** 1442–1479
    - **John Paston III** 1444–1504
    - **Margery Paston** c.1449–c. 1480, m. Richard Calle
    - **Edmund Paston II** c.1450–c.1500
    - **Anne Paston** c. 1455–1494
    - **Walter Paston** c.1457–v. 1479
    - **William Paston III** c. 1459–c. 1503
  - **Elizabeth Paston** c. 1429–c. 1488, m. 1) Robert Poynings 2) Sir George Browne
  - **William Paston II** c.1436–1496, m. Lady Anne Beaufort
  - **Clement Paston** 1441–c.1468

to fight hard and dirty to hold on to what he believed was his rightful inheritance. He showed very early on how he was going to set about his self-imposed (or perhaps father-imposed) task, by the way he acted when his father died. He moved with shocking speed to grab all the valuables his father had left, to make sure nobody else got a share of them, and he did his best to prevent his brothers and sister from inheriting as much of the family land as his mother thought his father had intended them to get.[4]

You might think from this that John Paston was not a very nice man, and I think you would be right. One interesting thing about Paston studies is that the family tend to get a rather good press from historians. Of course we are jolly grateful that successive generations of Pastons held on to all those old papers, and many people justifiably admire John Paston's wife Margaret's courage in the face of very difficult circumstances and her winning turn of phrase. There are some letters by other family members that draw our sympathy and a degree of affection too. But I think it is a mistake to get too sentimental about the family, because even by the standards of their time, they by no means always behaved admirably. We mostly get the Pastons' side of every story, since their opponents' side is long lost, and obviously they didn't write down and keep details of anything illegal they did. But even though we are reading their version of history, it is clear that some of the Pastons, and that certainly includes John Paston, did some things that were thoroughly nasty. So the story I am telling here is not of a fine, heroic figure, it is more a story of a little man thrust into a role too big for him, and behaving pretty grubbily at times in his efforts to live up to his position.

John Paston trained as a lawyer, like his father, and his main tactic for making money during the rest of his life was to do what his father seems to have done with some success, and induce his legal clients to leave their cash and land to him. He fixed in particular on Sir John Fastolf, who was related in some way to his wife; who was extremely rich, a whole level richer than John Paston and those other Norwich gentlepeople who figured in the taxation list; and who also had the great advantage from a fortune-hunter's perspective that he did not have an obvious heir. He did have a couple of nephews, but he does not seem to have been particularly keen on them, and there is no sign he seriously considered leaving his estate to either of them.

Fastolf had made most of his money in the Hundred Years War. He did not just do as well financially as other prominent captains, he seems to have done a lot better than most of them. He spent some of this fortune building one of the finest new castles in England at Caister in south-east Norfolk, and he also owned a huge spread of land not just in East Anglia but all down the length of Eastern England.

Fastolf's main plan for his estate during the last years of his life was to use it to set up a college of monks who would hold masses and send up prayers to ease his path through purgatory.[5] He had to get a licence from the king in order to do this, which was not cheap, and when it was clear it was not going to be agreed by the time he died, John Paston tried to persuade Fastolf to leave him the estate in return for his promise to set up the college.

This would have been a very good deal for John Paston, because the estate was worth far more than was needed to set up the college. But the problem was, Fastolf never signed any of the wills John Paston drew up. Paston was not deterred, though and when Fastolf died in 1459, Paston presented for probate an unsigned will, a nuncupative will in legal terms, which he claimed represented Fastolf's dying intentions. To say that this was a dubious move is putting it politely. It was frankly outrageous. Most of the East Anglian gentry and nobility certainly were outraged, and Fastolf's disinherited nephews seem to have been pretty put out too. But John Paston did not back down, and he spent the rest of his life trying to get this inheritance confirmed.

To be fair, he did set up the college of monks after a fashion. But what he did not do was to spread around his good fortune, and bribe all the other interested parties enough to persuade them to back him up. So the opposition he faced did not die down, and he and his family were confronted not only with legal attempts to over turn the nuncupative will, but also with physical attempts to take Fastolf's estates away from them.

One of the most notorious of these happened in 1465, the year before John Paston's death, when a troop of men put together by the duke of Suffolk seized and wrecked two of Fastolf's old estates at Hellesdon and Drayton. They demolished the manor houses, they terrorized the tenants, and they even sacked Hellesdon church. Perhaps many of the men who took part in this raid were old soldiers who forgot they were not still in France.[6]

Whatever the rights and wrongs of the Fastolf inheritance, this attack was appalling. John Paston was in London when it took place, but his wife Margaret seems only just to have left Hellesdon when the duke's men came. This was probably her main home at the time, just as Gresham had been 16 years earlier, so she twice experienced a large band of men descending on her home and trashing it.

Being attacked was not the only danger the Pastons faced. Their opponents could also argue that if John Paston did not validly own the Fastolf estates, he and his servants were committing theft in trying to collect rents on them or sell the produce from them. They were also committing trespass, simply by setting foot on them. John Paston was determined to uphold his claims, so he and his men did continue to try to administer and profit from the estates, and as they result they faced a long series of legal challenges and writs throughout the early 1460s. On at least one occasion John Paston was threatened with outlawry,[7] and he spent a number of spells in the Fleet Prison, including one that only ended shortly before his death.[8]

In fairness, going to jail in those days was not a sentence for a crime, it was what was done with men who were awaiting trial, and men who couldn't pay their creditors. We do not know all the details of the writs against John Paston, but it is pretty clear that as well as facing accusations of theft and trespass, he was also seriously in debt in his later years. He might have been one of the richest men in Norwich 15 years earlier, but the costs of defending all the attacks on him, both in the courts and on the ground, and the difficulties of getting income out of both the Paston and the Fastolf estates, meant that a lot of his money had gone by the mid-1460s. John Paston was regularly complaining about lack of money in that period, and his servants must have been complaining too, because there are mentions in the Papers of their pay being as much as a year in arrears.[9] John Paston was still land rich, but he seems at this point to have been cash poor. It is worth pointing out that he does not seem to have been convicted of any of the crimes he was accused of. Even so, men and women from respectable families tended not to spend months in jail, and I think this sorry saga left him with a very battered reputation.

One other issue was also proving a serious problem to the Pastons at this point in their fortunes: the status of their ancestors. It was widely thought in their own time, and is also generally believed by historians today, that the Pastons' near ancestors had been bondmen.

Caister Castle
(photo by the author)

The mid-15th century was the very dying days of the feudal system, and evidently his servile status did not do anything to stop Judge William from building his career. But when men were looking for mud to throw at John Paston, this was one of the lumps they picked up. And it was not just a question of damaging his reputation: if his enemies could have proved he was a bondman by birth, that gave them an additional reason to argue that he could not validly inherit the Fastolf estates.

Of course John Paston fought back against these allegations too, and reading between the lines, he did so in his usual none too ethical way. He put together a dossier of papers, including court rolls and deeds, to show that his family had been lords of the manor for many generations back in what they rather grandly called 'the town of Paston', and that far from being bondmen, they had owned bondmen themselves.[10] Since this does not appear to have been the case, I think the obvious conclusion is that they forged this dossier. John Paston and his wife were convinced that the rival claimants to their family estates had forged deeds to back up their own cases,[11] so he probably justified this to himself as a fair way of retaliating in the circumstances. His family submitted this grand dossier to King Edward IV, and they were still waiting for him to pronounce on its validity and, they hoped, to give them his explicit support, when John Paston died.

So the man who was given this lavish funeral was a complex and difficult character. From one perspective, we could view him a crooked lawyer who did his utmost to profit unethically out of his clients, and who spent a good chunk of his final years in jail. But from another perspective, he did manage to maintain a position in the upper ranks of East Anglian society. John Paston did not have the kind of stellar public career that his father had had, but that does not mean he had no public career at all. Pretty much any able-bodied landowner was expected to take on his share of public appointments, and John Paston did do so. He served on some commissions to look into incidents of disorder in Norwich, and he was a justice of the peace and on a couple of occasions a member of Parliament. These appointments seem to have dried up by the early 1460s, perhaps partly because Paston was preoccupied with his own troubles, and partly because his health was deteriorating. He was only 45 when he died.

The 'town of Paston'
(photo by the author)

Now we need to change perspective and look at the situation in which he left his family, and particularly his heir, who was also called John, although unlike his father he had accepted the knighthood he was offered, so by this time he was Sir John Paston.

Sir John was in his early 20s when his father died, much the age his father had been when his grandfather died, and he inherited a rather similar task. His family might have had two generations now of wealth and prominence, but it was in a seriously battered state when he took over as its head. And his task was to restore its reputation, and to do whatever he could to ensure that the family held on to at least some of the estates that his father had laid claim to.

I think we have to look at the details of the funeral firmly from this perspective. If the Pastons chose to put on a stonking funeral for John Paston, it was not out of sentiment. Even if they felt a great deal of grief (and there is not much sign of it, particularly from Sir John, who had been on very bad terms with his father for years), I don't think it helps to see their motive *primarily* in terms of doing the best they could possibly afford in memory of a great husband and father. Nor do I think we need to view their decisions through a prism of religion. The family seems to have been conventionally religious, but not obsessively so by the standards of their times. Of course religious conviction played a part, and at least some members of the family probably grieved sincerely for John Paston, but I think the core motive was a hard-headed assessment of what practical return they would get from their outlay.

But few people make their decisions entirely rationally, and it is worth pointing out one other motive. John Paston himself had been a tight-fisted man. Margaret Paston had complained repeatedly that she did not have clothes and jewels to match those that other rich women in Norwich wore,[12] and her sons always seem to have been short of cash when their father was alive. His eldest son was inclined in the other direction, he was a bit of a spendthrift.[13] So when Sir John got hold of the purse strings, I think he was temperamentally inclined to spend lots of money and give all the mourners a fine time, in a way that he knew his father would have hated. And his mother must have backed him up, or at least not opposed him when he chose to splash out.

So what did they hope to achieve? At the heart of everything there was the need to reinforce the family's position in society. The Pastons had a claim to being a major landowing family, one of the great families, at least in financial terms, in the East Anglia of their day, but as we have seen, this was a claim that had met with a great deal of opposition throughout John Paston's adult lifetime. So they could not take this social position for granted, and they needed to use the funeral to buttress it.

There were the Fastolf estates. John Paston died more than six years after Sir John Fastolf's death, but probate had still not been granted in Fastolf's will. So the family needed to use the funeral as a kind of PR exercise to underline their claim to the estates. At the same time, if they identified John Paston too much with the Fastolf lands, it was sure to enrage their opponents, so they had to give some thought to how best to achieve this.

And there was the dossier of papers they had submitted to the king. They must have been expecting the king to act in the near future on this dossier, which means they expected him to express his support for the family and their claims, and it would have been difficult for them when John Paston died before he had done this. They obviously did not expect the king to come to the funeral, but they would have expected him to hear about it, especially if they put on the kind of lavish show that got people talking and marked them out as rich and influential supporters of the kind that the king – indeed, both of the rival claimants to the throne – definitely needed.

So this is the core of it, I think. Sir John and his mother, and the rest of his family too, reckoned that it was important to give East Anglian society a firm message that they were a rich and powerful family, and that they were not backing down on any of their claims. And they were willing to pay out a large sum, probably a much larger sum than they could easily afford, in order to make sure this message got across.

We don't know exactly who made all the decisions, or did all the work of coordinating the funeral ceremonies, but probably all the leading Pastons had a hand in it. That means primarily Margaret, John Paston's widow; Sir John, his young heir; and William Paston II, his brother, who was by then a very successful lawyer in London. The living Pastons did not make all the decisions; they would have been guided by John Paston's own wishes and instructions. Men of his era gave a great deal of thought to their funerals and their legacies, and although as far as I know John Paston's will is lost, we can see his hand, for instance, in the entry in the list that reads 'To the Prior to meet the deceased's bequest'. This is the prior of Bromholm Abbey, which is in Bacton, the next village to Paston in north-east Norfolk, and its size, 40 shillings, probably reflects the fact that John Paston had decided to be buried at Bromholm.

He actually died in London. Another entry in the list reads 'To the keeper of the inn where John Paston died, for his reward.' The 20 shillings listed is a substantial sum, so we can guess that John Paston occupied a room in the inn for some time, probably for several days, perhaps even several weeks, before his death, and then after his death for as long as was needed to organize the procession that would bring his body to his burial place. John Paston spent much of his time in London based at the Inner Temple, as did his brothers William and Clement, and it is not clear whether the 'inn' mentioned was a common lodging house, or whether it was chambers at the Temple in which he had been lodging.

The Pastons

Making the decisions: the dead man's wife, son, brother (guided by his will).
Glass (not specifically representing the Pastons) from the church of St Peter and St Paul, East Harling.

obviously decided to bring the dead man back to Norfolk and not to see him buried in London. If they saw any arguments for choosing London, they must have thought the arguments for Norfolk were stronger. Whereabouts it should be in Norfolk was also an issue that must have taken some thought, because there were a number of options available to them.

Of course many families had an established burial place, where generations had been laid to rest. But the Pastons' situation was complicated, to put it mildly, not just by the obscurity of their ancestors, but by the documents they had produced to create a more distinguished lineage. That ancestry was based in Paston, as were their real ancestors, but it must have been quite tricky to square the actual bondsmen who would presumably have been buried in Paston churchyard with the fictional owners of bondmen they had dreamed up. It would not do to lay John Paston to rest alongside his real ancestors when the family had rewritten history so completely. And that was probably reason enough to rule out Paston church.

The Inns of Court, where John Paston spent much of his time.

The only ancestor of John Paston's (not counting his mother, who was still alive) whose burial place we know for certain was his father, the judge. He was buried in the Lady Chapel at Norwich Cathedral (which was destroyed at the Reformation), although actually he too had died in London.[14] But burial in the cathedral was the kind of honour that a man had to earn, and it would certainly have been a controversial, and probably an impossible, choice for a man like John Paston, who was not a distinguished judge but a recently released prisoner.

The grandest estate to which the Pastons laid claim was Caister, but it would have been provocative for John Paston to be buried there, and in fact Fastolf himself had not been buried in the castle chapel; his tomb was at St Benet's Abbey. The family's main seat outside the Fastolf inheritance was at Oxnead, but that was held by Agnes Paston, John Paston's mother, and he had probably never lived there, although that did become the standard burial place for later generations of the family.

Norwich was clearly an option, because that taxation list reflected the fact that the Pastons spent much of their time in the city. They had connections with a number of churches over the years, but their main connection was with St Peter Hungate, the parish in which they must have lived at this time. So there was some argument for John Paston's being buried here, or perhaps in one of the friary churches that the family had patronised.

But the strongest argument was clearly for Bromholm. I think the core reason is a simple one: the genealogy the Pastons had drawn up led straight back to the founding of

Bromholm. There is confirmation of this in one of the papers that details the dossier the family submitted to Edward IV:

> They shewed a lineall descent how their first ancetor Wulstan came out of France, and Sir William Glanville together, his kinsman, that after founded the pryory of Bromholme by the town of Paston and the towne of Bentley, and how Wulstan had issue Wulstan, which bare armes gould flowret azure, and how he had issue Raffe and Robert, which Raffe senior bare arms as his father and Robert the younger bare silver flowret asure. And Robert had issue Edmund and Walter, which Edmund the elder bare as his father, and his brother, because he married Glanviles daughter, a cheife indented golde, the field silver flowret azure; and how their ancetors bare with less number; and how Sir John Paston was heire to all those for they dyed sans issue. And this was shewed by writing of olde hand and by old testaments and evidences.[15]

It was a popular business in the 15th century to draw up this kind of genealogy, and many noble families had just as much fiction in theirs as the Pastons had in this one. Lots of people must have known it was a fiction, but it was a fiction they badly needed to make stick, and one good way to do this was to strengthen the family's supposed long association with Bromholm Priory.

There are only a few ruins of Bromholm Priory left today. It was a Cluniac house, and was sometimes also known as Bacton Abbey. It was founded in 1113 by William de Glanville, who was the lord of Bacton. The 14th-century Bromholm Psalter still survives in the Ashmolean. But the main claim to fame of the priory was that it possessed the 'holy cross of Bromholm', a part of the True Cross, which Chaucer and Langland both mentioned.

So this was a major place of pilgrimage, and a prestigious place for a man to be buried. Of course he had to earn that privilege, and we can read in many places in the funeral costs list exactly how the Pastons paid for it.

But if Bromholm was where John Paston's body ended up, it was not the only place it was taken. We can reconstruct from the expenses list and a few other mentions exactly how the Pastons planned the funeral.

They started off in London of course, and there is mention of two men waiting on John Paston for seven days, although it is not clear whether those days were all before his death, or included a day or two after it when the funeral arrangements were being made. Then a very formal procession set off to Norfolk, which included 12 poor men bearing torches, and a priest, plus servitors to wait on him. It also included a woman to tend the corpse and keep it from stinking too much, because he died around the end of May (the dates given in different sources vary from 21 to 25 May), so it would have been quite warm, and no doubt the smell was a serious problem. All these mourners were paid, and throughout the list are an assortment of payments, not just to workers who set things up, but also to religious officials who were called on to attend. In many cases this was dressed up as charity, but there is an obvious subtext here that if you did not pay up, these people did not come. I am not suggesting here that the Pastons did anything unusual, I think all this was pretty standard for their era.

The procession took six days to get from London to Norwich, so it moved slowly, with overnight stops. It might have included some of the family and their servants too, but probably not a great deal of them, because they were all needed in Norwich and Bromholm to make the arrangements for the rest of the ceremonial. We can see from the costs list that there was a huge amount of work, including preparing vestments for the people who took part in the services, apparently making tents which they would have needed in Bromholm to accommodate all the people who came to the interment who could not fit into the abbey guest accommodation, and not least, sorting out an enormous amount of food.

We do not know the exact route it took, and the list isn't a great deal of help here, because the donations listed are many of them to establishments in which the Pastons certainly had an interest, but which were not necessarily along the funeral route. Obviously a procession like this would want to keep to a main road, but they might well have diverted a little to ensure that it went through some of the Fastolf estates, places such as Cotton in Suffolk, where the Pastons had had quite a bit of trouble, and it would have been useful to bring out the troops, as it were, and make sure everyone saw this demonstration of wealth and power.

Norwich is on the natural route to Bromholm, but clearly it was not just a stopping-off point, or a point to collect some of the family for the last stages of the journey, it was seen as a destination in its own right. There was a major service in St Peter Hungate, and probably a lot of people saw or participated in the ceremonies in Norwich but did not make the long trek out to Bromholm. So I think we have to see the Norwich phase as a very significant part of the whole PR exercise that this funeral partly represented.

When the procession approached Norwich, representatives of the four orders of friars that had houses in the

The journey home: from London to Bromholm via Norwich

St Peter Hungate, Norwich

city rode out to meet it. And naturally these were paid too, or at least donations were given which amounted to a form of payment. Then the bells were rung, apparently at both St Peter Hungate and St Stephen, and that too would have made sure as many people as possible knew this huge funeral was taking place, so it spread the message behind the Pastons' major effort and expenditure.

The corpse was then set in St Peter Hungate, let us hope in a closed coffin since it was a good week now since John Paston had died, and there was a 'dirge'. This was not a funeral mass, but obviously it was a major service of mourning with music involved. And it is clear from the accounts that a very large cast of paid attendees was assembled for this. Presumably the family and many of their servants, tenants and friends were there as well.

They must have been particularly keen to get the prioress of Carrow Abbey, since they had to pay a large donation to her and her maid. Then they brought along 23 sisters from the Norman Hospital plus their warden, 38 priests, 39 children with the surplices that had been run up in the days beforehand, who were stationed both inside and outside the church, singers, 26 clerks and four keepers of the torches. The poor men and the woman tending the corpse who had come from London would have been there too. St Peter is not a huge church, so it must have been very crowded, and it is particularly interesting to notice that because it was so full of people and the Pastons had so many candles lit, they had to arrange for a glazier to take out some of the window glass to let out the fumes, and put it back afterwards.

This was not the funeral proper, it was just a warm-up, and after the dirge the whole procession, probably enlarged considerably from the group who had set out from London, started out again, on the journey to Bromholm. They would not have made Bromholm in a day moving at funeral pace, so perhaps the three days that they paid for a horse for the family chaplain, Sir James Gloys, is an indicator of how long it took to get there. And as you can see, the Pastons' servants and men of business brought along money to dispense as alms to the poor people who must have come out to watch this procession pass by. By this point I guess no one would have envied the corpse-tender her job.

We can see from the list that workmen had started assembling at Bromholm five days before the interment, with the group of them being added to day by day. Bromholm was quite a big establishment, but clearly it could not put on this kind of a show without external help. And just as at Norwich, the funeral in Bromholm involved an enormous cast of priests, servitors and bellringers. There were also lots of workmen who set up the infrastructure before hand, and servants who looked after the most important guests, made sure everyone got fed and so on. The day of the funeral itself they seem to have had a meat-oriented meal, and many of the people who had come were clearly still there the day afterwards, when a fish meal was served up to them before they all dispersed.

We do not know from the list of expenses, but we do know from other documents where exactly John Paston was buried in the priory church. Sir John Paston, John Paston's son, wrote to ask his brother in 1471:

> I wolde fayne haue the mesure wher my fadre lythe at Bromholm, both the thykness and compase off the peler at hys hed and from that the space to the alter, and the thyknesse off that awtre and jimagery off tymbre werk, and what hyught the arche is to the ground off the jlde, and how hye the grovnde off the quyre is hyer than the grownde off the ilde.[16]

There is a little more information in Sir John's will, which specifies that if he dies in Norfolk, he should be buried at Bromholm, 'ny unto the founders tombe, which arche is unto the northsyde and ryght agayn my fadyre tombe'. He suggested a fairly modest £20 would be sufficient to pay for his tomb and an adjoining altar. Note that mention of the founder's tomb: obviously it was important to the Pastons to make the connection with Sir William Glanville as emphatically as they could.

It is interesting to note that Sir John did not want his own body to be hauled up to Norfolk if he died in London. He specifically put it into his will that if he died in London, that was where he was to be buried.[17]

Of course, the observation of a medieval death was not complete with the funeral and the reading of the will. As well as regular masses to pray for the soul of the dead person

Bromholm Priory

(which we can see were done for John Paston until the Michaelmas after the year of his death), there was a ceremony to mark 30 days after the death, another on the anniversary of the death, and a light was kept burning on the tomb. And a surprisingly small amount was paid to the vicar of Dalling, only 8s 4d to get him all the way to Rome and back, so perhaps he supplemented that with payments from other families for which was doing errands.

Let me close by looking briefly at what happened after John Paston's funeral. Did all this expense achieve what it was intended to? It is true that Fastolf's will was probated broadly in the Pastons' favour, and that they did hold on to Caister Castle for a while, though they later lost it. And King Edward IV did indeed accept the package of papers that had been submitted to him, and the Pastons' claims about their genealogy. He issued a proclamation to the bailiffs of Yarmouth and other places in July 1466, only a couple of months after the funeral, confirming this. Part of it reads:

> that the tenants, baylies, fermors, and occupiers of [the Fastolf lands] ... duely and hooly pay to the said Sir John Paston the hoole issues, proffits thereof as ye did unto his father at any time in his life; and that ye mayers, shreves, eschetors and other our officers, and all ye tenants, fermors, baylies, and occupiers of any of the lands and tenements aforesaid, ... be assisting, helping and strengthening unto the said Sir John Paston and to [his family].
>
> 'By the Kinge Edward the Fourth', 26/27 July 1466[18]

To the Pastons, this maybe genuinely was worth the equivalent of a million pounds in today's money.

But their money problems did not come to an end, and although they did not stint on John Paston's funeral, the Pastons certainly did stint on completing the tomb afterwards. For instance Margaret Paston, his widow, wrote to her son Sir John in November 1471:

> Yt is a schame, and a thyng that is myche spokyn of in thys contre, that yowr faders graue ston is not mad. Fore Goddys loue, late yt be remembyrd and purveyde fore in hast–there hathe be myche more spend in waste than schuld haue mad that.[19]

Some of us might be tempted to class some of the funeral expenses among that spending in waste, though there is no reason to think that is what she was referring to.

As I mentioned earlier, Sir John seems to have been an extravagant man, and after his father was dead, his mother got the job of complaining about it. But if his mother thought this was all his fault, he in turn seemed to think it was her fault, because a couple of years later he wrote to his brother:

> I preye yow remembre hyre [my mother] for my fadrys tombe at Bromholme. She dothe ryght nott; I am afferde off hyre that she shall nott doo weell.[20]

Whoever's fault it was, it is very clear that both Sir John and his mother found it impossible to carry out all the instructions in John Paston's will. In November 1471, five and a half years after his death, Margaret wrote to her son that:

> I woold he [the archbishop of Canterbury] schuld be informyd wat scharge and lossesys we haue had that hath causyd the godys to be spent so that we be not abyl to perform hys [JP's] wyll ....[21]

Sir John evidently wanted to receive a discharge, a confirmation that he had completed execution of the will, and it must have been pretty embarrassing that he could not afford to, or perhaps just would not, meet all its requirements.

Another interesting snippet concerns the cloth of gold I mentioned, which seems to have covered John Paston's coffin. When the duke of Norfolk died suddenly in January 1476, Sir John wrote to his mother about it:

> And it is soo that thys contré is nott weell purveyd off cloth off gold for the coveryng for hys bodye and herse, whereffor, euery man helpyng to hys powere, I put the cowncell off my lorde in cownfforte that I hopyd to gete on for that day if it weer so that it be nott broken or putt to other vse. Wherffor please it yow to sende me worde iff it be so that ye have or kan komby the clothe of tyssywe that I bowte for my faderys tombe; and I vndertake it shall be saffyd agaeyn for yowe on-hurt at my perell. I deme hereby to gete gree thanke and greet assystence in tyme to come ...[22]

It is not clear whether the cloth of gold ever reached the duke of Norfolk's coffin, but if it did, it came safely back to the Pastons afterwards. Because two years later, Margaret was sending it to Sir John again. But this time, she was determined that if he sold it, he was to use the profits to finish the work on John Paston's tomb, which was still uncompleted out at Bromholm. So when he got it from the carrier Wheatley, she wanted him to send her word in writing. And she added to him,

> Yf ye sellyt to any othyr vse, by my trowthe I zall neuer trost yow wyll I leue. Remembyr that yt coste me 21 marke the pleggyng owte of yt ...[23]

Pledging out: obviously the Paston's money problems were still pretty acute, because that sounds as if she had had to bring it out of pawn. And she added some more about other families who had buried their dear departed at Bromholm:

> My cosyn Clere[24] dothe as meche coste at Bromholm as whylle drawe an cli. upon the deskys in the quere and in othyr places, and Heydon in lyke whyse, and if there xulde no thyng be done for your father, yt wolde be to gret a schame for vs alle, and in chieffe to see hym lye as he dothe ... [25]

So had the Pastons established themselves as the major patrons of Bromholm Priory? It looks as if, as happened all too often, they were never really able to follow through from the great extravagance of the funeral, and that they were not proving nearly as generous patrons as some far less prominent families. The monks and pilgrims at Bromholm can have been none too impressed as poor John Paston continued to lie beneath his unfinished – and long since lost – tomb.

Susan Curran *is a freelance writer and editor, whose historical books include* The English Friend, The Marriage of Margery Paston *and* The Wife of Cobham. *She is proprietor of the Lasse Press, and a trustee of the Norwich Historic Churches Trust.*

Notes

References are to the two volumes of Norman Davis's edition of the *Paston Letters and Papers of the Fifteenth Century* (Oxford: Clarendon Press, vol. 1, 1971 and vol. 2, 1976), given here as D1 and D2 respectively.

1. For instance, Walter Aslak's complaints against him are in D2, p. 505.
2. The friar who claimed Oxnead is mentioned e.g. in Agnes Paston's letter, D1, p. 31.
3. The loss in particular is covered extensively in the letters, e.g. D1, pp. 225–33. (The recovery is apparent from later letters.)
4. His mother's account is in D1, p. 46.
5. There are various drafts of Fastolf's will, e.g. D1, pp. 87–91.
6. The attacks are mentioned extensively, e.g. D1, pp. 323–4.
7. See D2, p. 545.
8. Many mentions, e.g. Sir John writes to his father in the Fleet, D1, p. 395.
9. See land agent Richard Calle's complaints, D2, p. 395.
10. Edward IV's summary of these documents is in D2, p. 551–2 (quote from p. 551).
11. D1, p. 231.
12. One famous comment is in D1, p. 250.
13. Among Margaret Paston's complaints about her son's extravagance is D1, p. 352.
14. D2, p. 609.
15. D2, p. 552.
16. D1, p. 442.
17. D1, p. 506.
18. D2, pp. 549–50.
19. Margaret Paston to Sir John Paston, November 1471: D1, p. 359.
20. Sir John Paston to his brother John Paston III, 1473. D1. p. 458.
21. Margaret Paston to Sir John Paston, 20 November 1471, D1, p. 358.
22. Sir John Paston to Margaret Paston, 17 January 1476, D1, pp. 489–90.
23. Margaret Paston to John Paston, 27 May 1478, D1, p. 380.
24. This is almost certainly the Elizabeth Clere who also figured in the 1451 taxation list.
25. Margaret Paston to John Paston, 27 May 1478, D1, p. 380.

Index

Illustrations are indicated with **bold** print. Saints are indexed under their given names. Notes are indexed in the format 47n144 for note 144 on page 47.

A

Acton, Thomas, 54
advowsons, 74–5, 76
Aethelthryth, St, 7
Agatha, St, 4, 6
Allen, William, 50
altars
   altarpieces, 67
   position of, 38
anchorites/anchoresses, 16, 84
Anderson, M. D., 9
Andrews, William Eusebius, 54
Angier, Thomas, 56
Anne, St, 21
Antingham church, 80
Apollonia, St, 2–7
Appleyard, Sir John, 51
Ashby church, 10
Ashmole, Elias, 65
Ashwellthorpe triptych, 24
aspergement, 30–1, 45n104
Audrey, St, 7
augmentation, 29
aumbries, 20, 29, 41n24
Aylsham church, 23

B

Babingley church, 4
Bacon, Nathaniel, 30, 35–6
Baker, John, 17
banners and banner stave cupboards, 33
Barbara, St, 23
Bardolf, William, 77
Barker, John, 25
Barton, Andrew, 69
Barton, John jr, 63, 66–7, 68–9
Barton, John sr, 61–71
Barton, Ralph, 68
Barton Turf church, 4, **5**
Batchcroft, Thomas, 32
Bawburgh, 31, 47n144
Beauchamp, Richard, bishop of Salisbury, 11
Beaumont, Edward, 55–6

Bedingfield, Sir Henry, 54
beguinages, 16
bells, 4, 9, 24, 43n56, 45n100, 45n101, 101–2
   angelus, 30
   ringers, 84
   sanctus, 30
bench ends, 23, 67
Benstead, Thomas, 52
Beza, Theodore, 29–30, 37
Bible
   Bishops' Bible, 34
   Great Bible, 34, 47n146
   texts from, 4, 26, 34, 64
Bingham family, 62
Binham
   church, 4, 34, **36**
   Priory, 12
Bintree church, 80, 81n28
Bird, Henry, 34, **35**
Blomefield, Francis, 21, 31, 47n143, 81
Blue Nuns, 56
Boleyn, Sir William, 7
Borrow, George, 56
Bossy, John, 49
boundaries, land, significance of, 31–2
Bownd, Nicholas, 36
Bowthorpe church, 79, 81n25
Brandon church, 80, 81n28
brasses, 21, 23, 42n29
   Virgin on, 23
Brigg, John, 18
Brinton church, 1
Bromholm Priory, 32, 84–7, 98–103, **103**
Bromholm Psalter, 100
Broom church, 77
Burlingham St Edmund, 17
Burnham Deepdale, 46n136
Burnham Norton church, 17
Bury St Edmunds, 56
   Abbey (ruins), 54
   Cathedral, 35
Butler, Alban, 54, **55**

C

Caister, Richard, 23, 24
Caister Castle, 93, **95**, 99, 104
Calthorpe, Lady, 26
Calvin, John/Calvinism, 29

INDEX

candles, 6, 23, 26, 27, 86, 88–9, 102
Capp, Thomas, 23
Carlisle, Andrew Harclay, earl of, 79–80
Carr, James, 56
Castle Acre, St James's church, 17
Castle Hedingham, 18
Castle Rising, 77
Catherine, St, 23
Cawston church, 12, 17, 18, 21
certiorari writ, 74–5, 78
chantries, 7, 16, 23, 24, 26, 27
  screens surrounding, 33–4, 63
charity, 16, 84–9, 101–3
  see also donors
chrism, the, 29
Church (of England), post-reformation preoccupations/theology of, 34–9, 50
Church, pre-Reformation
  criticisms of, 19
  preoccupations/theology of, 19–29
church buildings
  amalgamation and loss, 18–19
  personalized space within, 27 (*see also* donors)
  phases of alteration (not rebuilding), 19
  phases of rebuilding, 17, 18
  proprietorial attitudes to, 21, 27
  rehistoricizing of, 39
  ringing chambers, 33
  under-arches, 30–1, 45n104
  west doors, 33
  see also bench ends, fonts, rood screens, seating, stained glass, individual churches by name
Clenchwarton, 77, 81n28
Clere, Elizabeth, 90, 105, 106
Clerk, Gregory, 24
Cley church, 4
Clopton family, 18
Cock, John, 23
Cokeruill, Frederick, 77
Colby church, **37**
College of the Holy Apostles, 52–4
communion, **28**
  magical properties of, 28–9
  post Reformation practice, 35
  tables, 37
  vessels, 20, 27, 29, 35, **37**
  see also mass
Compton, Henry, bishop of London, 53
Costessey Hall, **51, 52**
Cotman, John Sell, 23
Cotton, Richard, 54

Cotton (Suffolk), 101
Cranach, Lucas (the elder), 3
Cringleford, 31, 47n144
Cromer church, 1
crosses
  external statuary, 31–2
  festival of the cross, 32
  holy cross of Bromholm, 100
  market crosses, 31
  palm crosses, 32
  processional, 33
cults
  implications of, 26–7
  of Jesus, 25–6
  of the Virgin, 23–5

D

Dalling, vicar of, 103
Dante Alighieri, 21, 30
Day, John, 38
debate, theological, 19
Dent church, 79–80
Dersingham church, 4
Despencer, Henry, 41
diet, medieval
  food for funerals, 85–7, 103
  impact on teeth, 1
Docking church, 6
doctrine, definition, 19
dogma, definition, 19
donors, to medieval churches, 6–7, 18–19, 24, 32, 43n67, 44n78, 61–71
  material evidence of identity, 18, 32, 61–72
  represented in stained glass, 21, **22**, 65, 69
Dorothea of Casesarea, 23
Dorothy, St, 23
drama, medieval, 3, 32
Drayton, 94
Duffy, Eamon, 4

E

Eagle, Lincs, 62
East Barsham
  church, 43n61
  Hall, 18
East Harling church, 33, 47n140, **98**
Edward IV, king, 62, 96, 97–8, 104
Edward VI, king, 3, 37
election, concept of, 30
Elizabeth I, queen, 21, 50–1
Ellys, Anthony, 69
Elsing church, 29

Ely
  Cathedral, 6, 7, 8
  St Etheldreda's, 8
Erpingham, Sir Thomas, 26, 32, 44n78
Erpingham chasuble, 26
escheators, 73, 75–6, 77, 80n1
Esyngwold, Richard, 12
Ethedreda, St, 7–8
Etreville, Thomas d', 56
Eye church, 9

F
Fastolf, Sir John, 93–4, 97, 99
feudal system, 91, 94–5
Fewster, Mary, 35
Fincham, inquisition at, 77
fonts, 8–10
  font covers, 38–9
  security of, 29
  seven-sacrament, 41n20
food *see* diet
Foulsham church, 80
Fouquet, Jean, 3
Foxe, John, 34
France, refugees from, 56
friars, 17
Friends of the Norwich Historic Churches Trust, v
funerals, 31, 83–9, 100–06
  procession, 100, 103

G
Galloway, Edward, 49, 56
Gateley church, **8**, 12, **13**
Genevieve, St, 3
Glanville, Sir William, 100, 103
Goldwell, James, 23
graffiti, in churches, 29
Great Ponton, 69
Great Snoring, 18
Great Witchingham church, 10
Greenway, John, 69, 70
Gresham, 91, 94
guilds/gilds
  of barber-surgeons, 2
  chantry chapels for, 16
  dedicated saints of, 7, 10
  feasts, 37
  Jesus guild, 26
  levies on, 7
  and processions, 31
  ritual objects owned/provided by, 27

  of St Mary, 24
  of St William, 10

H
Hamlet, 19
Harcocke, Edmund, 51
Harley-Smith, R., 61
Harryes, Robert, 12
Haveringland, 8, 9, 10
Hellesdon, 94
Hengham church, 80, 81n28
Henry VI, king, 11
Henry VII, king, 1
Henry VIII, king, 1, 12, 37
heraldry
  Christological, 26
  shown in churches, 18, 62, 68, 69
hermits, 16
High Church, 39
Hingham church, 6, 42n46
Hockering, 77
Hockwold church, 77
Holme by Newark, 61–2
  John Barton's house, 62, 71n7
  St Giles church, 61–72, **61**, 62–9, **63**
Holt, Geoffrey, 49
Holy Helpers, 21–2
Holy Kin, 21, 43n61
Hornyold, Bishop John Joseph, 56
Horsham, St Faith's church, 4, 17
Horstead, 31
Houghton St Giles, 43n61
houses
  constructed by rich merchants, 62, 69
  country, as palimpsests and time capsules, 17
  rebuilding of, 40n4
Husenbeth, Frederick, 54

I
Ickburgh church, 1
inquisitions post mortem, 73–82
intercessors/intercession
  in heaven, 21–2, 65–6
  living people as, 21
  priests as, 35
  saints as, 2–3, 7
  and totemic objects, 27
  the Virgin as, 23–4
Islington church, 77

J
James II, king, 54

Jannys, Robert, 69
Jerningham family, 51–2, 56
Jesuits, 52–4, 56–7
Jesus
  chapels, 26
  cult of, 25–6
Jews, 9
John, Bishop of Oxford, 32
Julian of Norwich, 16
juries, 73, 76

K

Kerdiston, Sir Thomas, 27
Kettlestone church, 78
Keyser, C. E., 10
King's Lynn *see* Lynn
knight's fees, 74–5, 78
Krikemer, Beatrix, 28

L

Latimer, Hugh, bishop of Worcester, 12, 34
Laud, William, archbishop, 39
Lavenham church, 33
Legenda Aurea, 2
Legge, Thomas, 35
Lessingham church, 4
Litcham church, 9, 27
Little Burgh church, 80
liturgy
  Catholic vs protestant, 50
  definition, 19
  Easter, 32, 33, 46n135
  see also communion; mass; services, divine
Loddon church, 9, **10**
Lollards, the, 19, 41n20
Lomynour, Robert, 25–6
London
  Inner Temple, 98, **99**
  St Etheldreda's, Ely Place, 8
Long Melford church, 18
Ludham church, 4
Luther, Martin/Lutheranism, 29
Lynn, 7, 10, 45n100

M

Mapping the Medieval Countryside Project, 75
Martin, Thomas, 4
Martyn, Roger, 18, 21
Mary, Queen, 52
Mary, St (the Virgin), 21
  cult of, 23–5
  chapels to, 23, 24, 63–7
  girdle of, 24, 28, 44–5n91
  images of, 31
  Seven Sorrows of, 24
mass
  changing practice in, 46–7n138
  funding of masses, 30, 32, 89, 93, 103
  see also communion, liturgy
Melton Constable church, 30
merchant's marks, 18, **66**, 68, 69
Milner, Bishop John, 56
miracles, claimed, 9, 11, 12
misericords, 1
Molyneaux, Catherine, 68
Monmouth, Thomas of, 8, 9
monuments, church, *see* brasses, tombs and monuments
More, John, 36
Morle, Robert, 80
Mumford, James, 53

N

Necton church, 78, 81n28
Nichols, S. M., 59
Norfolk, earls and dukes of, 50–1, 55–6, 80, 105
  Duke's Palace Norwich, **50**, 51
Norfolk, Mary, countess of, 80
Norfolk Museums Service, 4
North Creake church, **20**
North Elmham church, 1
North Marston, Bucks, 11
North Tuddenham church, 80, 81n28
North Walsham church, 37
Norwich
  All Saints Ber Street, 17
  All Saints Timberhill, 33
  Austin friars, 16, 44n78
  Blackfriars, 10, 15–16, 17, 23, 32, 33, 47n143
  boundaries of jurisdiction, 32
  Carrow Priory, 16, 24, 33, 43n59 (prioress, 84, 102)
  Cathedral (Anglican), 1, 4, 6, 7, 9, 10, 23, 24, 26, 35 (Carnary, 26, 42n50; Close, 16, 31, 32, 45n101; Holy Cross chapel, 32; Lady chapel, 99; shrine of St William, 9)
  Catholic Cathedral, 49, 57, **59**
  Catholic chapels, 49–60 (attacked, 54)
  Catholic community, 49
  Chapel in the Fields, 31

Chapel of St William, 9
Chapelfields, 54, 56
Charing Cross, 31
civic ordinances, 31
crosses, public, 31–2
Dominican Priory, 54
Duke's Palace, **50**, 51, 54
Duke's Place, 54–6, **55**
Earlham bridge, 32
Elizabeth I in, 51
Erpingham Gate, 6, 8, 26
friaries, 15–16, 101
Great Hospital, 15
Greyfriars, 16
guilds, 10, 16, 45n126
Harford bridges, 32
houses of religious fraternities, 32
inns, 20, 26
John Paston's dirge in, 84, 88, 101–2
Lamb Inn, 26, 44n77
Lollards' Pit, 41n20
lost medieval churches, 18–19 (*see also* individual churches by name)
market cross, 31
material culture of change visible in, 15–48
mayors, 69
medieval structure, 1516
Old Library, 29
ruling elite of, 30
St Andrew's, 26, 34, 36, 37, 39, 43n67, 44n79, 47n147
St Augustine's, 4, 32
St Benedict's Street, 17
St Crowche's, 31, 32
St Edmund's, 34, 47n144
St Etheldreda's, 8
St George Colegate, 31, 69
St Giles's church, 24, 31
St Giles's Hospital, 23, 42n50
St Gregory's, 30, 43n67, 69
St James, Pockthorpe, 8, 9, 24, 43n56, 43n57
St John and Holy Sepulchre, 36
St John Maddermarket, 9, 17, 21, 24, 26, 30, 31, 33, 44n75, 47n141 (Catholic chapel of, 56, **57**)
St Leonard's Priory, 24, 43n60
St Margaret Westwick, 25
St Martin in the Bailey, 31
St Martin at Oak, 24, 31, 33
St Martin at Palace Plain, 26
St Mary Coslany, 36
St Mary in the Fields, 16, 24, 42n51

St Mary the Less, 33
St Mary Magdalene, 8, 9
St Michael Berstreet, 10
St Michael/Miles Coslany, v, 10, 24, 33, 42n52
St Michael at Plea, 24, 31, 33
St Peter Hungate, 4, 24, 84, 88, 89, 99, 101, **102**
St Peter Mancroft, 8, 16, 21, **22**, **25**, 26, 29, 30, 32, 33, 43n64, 45n104
St Peter Southgate, 41n22, 44n79
St Stephen's, 4, **6**, 17, 21, **23**, 24–5, 28, 31, 32, 84, 102
St Swithin's Lane, 56
SS Simon and Jude, 24, 31
Shoulder of Mutton Yard, 54
Strangers' Hall, 35, 56
surviving medieval churches, v (*see also* individual churches by name)
taxation list, 90
Ten Bell Lane, 56
'Valuation of Norwich', 78
Whitefriars, 16
Willow Lane, 32, 45n125, 56 (Chapel, 56–7, **58**)
Norwich, bishops of, 23, 31, 41, 78, 79
Norwich Historic Churches Trust, v, 8

O
Oxnead, 91, 99

P
paintings
 featuring St Apollonia, 3
 on rood screens *see* rood screens
 of text, 36
 wall, 3, 10, 36–7
parclose screens, 33–4, 63
Paston, Agnes, 90, 91, 99
Paston, Sir John (jr), 97, 103–5
Paston, John sr, 83–106
Paston, Margaret, 93, 94, 97, 104
Paston, William jr, 85, 98
Paston, William sr, 91, 96, 99
Paston family
 family tree, 92
 feudal status, 95–6, 99, 104
 involvement in JP's funeral, 98
 reputation, 97
 servants, 84–6, 94, 101, 103
 wealth, 90–1, 94, 104–5
Paston letters, 83, 94

Paston (village), **96**, 99
Patience, James, 56
patronage
  of church buildings and fitments *see* donors
  of livings, 76–7, 80
personalization of religion, 27–8
Petre family, 52
pews, box, 39
Philip II of Spain, king, 3
Picton, J. W., 49
pilgrim badges, 11, 17, 24, 42n34, 44n84, 44–5n91
pilgrimages, 11–12, 17, 24, 31, 32
  payment for, 12
piscinae, **20**, 29, 41n22
porches (church), 18, 68–9
Poringland, Richard, 44n82
Potter Heigham church, 42n46, 46n132
prayers
  inscribed invocations, 21
  for intercession to ease toothache, 2
  intercession to speed the dead to heaven, 21, 71, 93
  learning by heart, 36–7
  prayer boards, 36–7
  requested on monuments, 18, 66
  to the Virgin, 23
preaching *see* sermons
predestination, 29
prison, 94
privacy, attitudes to, 17
  privatization of church space, 39
processions, religious, 30–3
purgatory, concept of, 18, 20–1, 23, 29, 53

Q
quarter days, 20

R
Radcliffe family, 68–9
Ranworth
  antiphoner, 21
  church, 8, 21
Reepham church, 24
Reformation
  degree of theological change, 19, 29–30, 34–9
  hostility to, 50
  implications for church buildings and fitments, 17–19, 34–9, **38**
relics
  of St Apollonia, vi, **3**
  of Christ and the Virgin, 44–5n91
  of St Edmund, 34
  of St Etheldreda, 7
  of St William, 9
  second-tier, 47n144
Reynes, Robert, 2
Richard III, king, 7, 11
Roman Catholic church (post Reformation), 35–6
  chapels in Norwich, 49–60
  Relief Acts, 49
  size of, 53, 56
rood screens, 33–4, **36**, 47n139
  at Holme by Newark, 63
  invocations inscribed on, 21, 35–6
  John Schorn represented on, 12
  St Apollonia represented on, 3–4, **5**
  St Etheldreda represented on, **8**
  St William represented on, 9, **10**
Rossi, Anthony, 49
Roughton church, 1, **2**
Rugge, Roger and Elizabeth, 23

S
saints
  and the Holy Kin/Helpers, 21–2
  local to Norwich *see* Caister, Richard; Edmund, St; Schorn, John; William, St
  prayers to, 2
  see also individual saints by name
Salle Church, 8, 17, 18, 29, 43n67
salvation, preoccupation with, 19
Sandringham church, 4
Sandys, Frederick, **20**
Sankey, Francis, 53
Scales, Robert de, 77
Schorn, John, 11–12
Schorn Book of Hours, 12
seating, in churches, 17, 39, 67
  sedilia, 20
Sedbergh church, 79–80
sermons and preaching, 12
  post Reformation, 34, 36
  preachers available in Norwich, 17
service, divine
  open air, 32, 33
  service books, 25, 31
  three new orders, 25
  see also communion, funerals, liturgy, mass
Shelton church, 21
Shipdham church, 36
Shotesham

All Saints church, **74**, 79
  St Martin's church, **79**
  St Mary's church, **78**, 81n24
Silver, Ferdinand, 54
Skeet, Ralph, 33
Smith, Richard, 53
Solomon, judgement of, **38**
Somerleyton church, 4
soteriology, 19
South Burlingham church, 17
South Walsham church, 21, 23–4
Southwold church, 1, 37
Speyne, Thomas, 23
Stafford, John, 54
Stafford, Nathaniel, 53–4
stained glass, 11, **98**
  donor figures in, 21
  at Holme by Newark, **65–7**, 68
  St Apollonia represented in, 3–4, **6**
  St William of Norwich represented in, 9
Stanhope, John, 68
Staple, the, 61–2, 68, 69
Stedman, Julian, 27
Stiffkey church, 4, 6
stone carvings,
  of people with toothache, 1, **2**
  St Apollonia represented in, 3–4
Strangers, 51
Sudbury church, 12
Suffield, Walter of, bishop of Norwich, 78, 79
Suffield church, 12
Suffolk, duke of, 94
Swaffham church, 36, 80
Swannington church, 29
symbolism
  conscious, of religious buildings, 15
  for men at arms, 26

T
talismans, 27, 28
taxation, 78–9, 90
teeth, quality of medieval people's, 1
textiles, 3–4, 24, 27
  altar frontals, 33
  bier cloths and palls, 27, **70**, 83, 105
  Westgate pall, 69, **70**
  see also vestments
Thetford
  Priory, 43n61
  St Etheldreda's, 7–8
Thoroton, Robert, 62
Thorp, Henry de, 76–7

Thorp, Robert, 24
Thorpe-next-Haddiscoe, 4
Tilney, 77, 78
Tiverton, 69, **70**
tombs and monuments, 7
  at Bromholm Priory, 103–5
  destruction prohibited, 21
  and the Easter sepulchre, 32
  funeral palls, 18, 69, **70**, 83, 105
  invocations inscribed on, 21
  of John Barton, **63–5**
  of Lady Calthorpe, 26
  location in churches, 20
  of Sir William Boleyn, 7
  see also brasses
Tony, Robert de, 78
toothache, 1–14
  representations of people with, 1, **2**,
  saints interceding for sufferers, 2–13
  treatments for, 1–2
toothdrawers, 2
Toppes, Robert, 21, **22**
totemism, 28, 44n83
Tottington church, 24
transubstantiation, 28
Trunch church, 29
Tudor, Mary, 1
typology, 37
Tyzard, John, 12

V
valuations of churches, 73–82
Vere family, 18
vestments, 33
  Bircham cope, 33, **34**, 46n136
  Holy Helpers on, 22–3
  for the Paston funeral, 101, 102
  St Apollonia represented on, 3, 6
  the Virgin on, 24
Victoria and Albert Museum, 3, 4, 9, 33, 67
Virgin *see* Mary
Virgoe, Roger, 90

W
wages, typical late medieval, 83, 90
Wakeryng, Bishop John, 31
Walpole St Peter, 33, 37, 38, 48n162
Walsingham, Shrine, **3**, 24
Walsoken church, 37, **39**
Walstan, St, 31
wardship, royal, 73, 75–7
Waxham church, 79, 80

Wells Cathedral, 1
Wells next the Sea, 78
West Walton church, 37, 48n157
Westgate, John, 18, 41n16, 69, 70
Westminster Abbey, 7
White, Thomas, 53
Wiggenhall St Mary, 24, 38
Wilby church, 48n165
William, St (of Norwich), 8–10, 43n62
wills, 30
  charitable/religious bequests in, 12, 21, 26, 27–8, 31
  of John Barton jr, 63
  of John Barton sr, 62, 63–4
  of John Paston sr, 98, 104
  of Sir John Paston, 103
  nuncupative of Sir John Fastolf, 93–4, 97, 104
Windsor, St George's Chapel, 11, 12
Wodehouse, John, 26
Wolferton church, 4
Wolsey, Thomas, 12
women
  nuns, 24, 56
  religious life of lay, 16, 25, 27
Woodhouse, Francis, 36
Wootton, 77
Worcester Cathedral, 7
Worstead church, 9, 46n132
Wren, Bishop Matthew, 39
writs, 74–5, 94
Wulstan, St, 47n144

Join the Friends
of the Norwich Historic Churches Trust

Why not join a convivial group that works to support Norwich's wonderful heritage of redundant churches? We fundraise to support the Norwich Historic Churches Trust which manages many of the churches, and organize regular events for members.
  Learn more, and download a membership form, from our website:

www.fnhct.org.uk

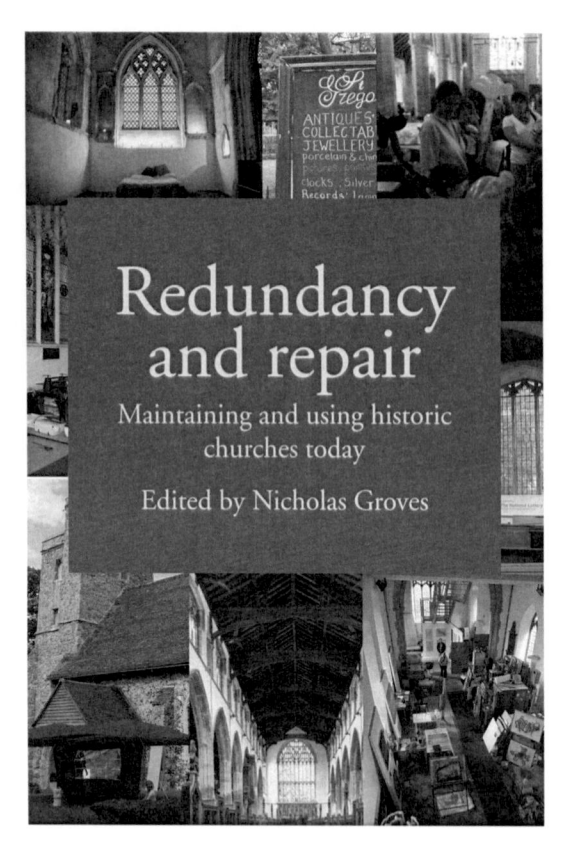

The Lasse Press's second collaboration with the Norwich Historic Churches Trust also draws on papers from its 2014 and 2015 conferences, supplemented by two papers on the history and experiences of the trust. It looks at issues related to the current use and maintenance of both active and redundant historic churches, with contributors from the Churches Conservation Trust, the Society for the Protection of Ancient Buildings, and independent researchers.

Provisional contents:

With concern, but not without hope: an overview of NHCT *Nicholas Groves*
Forging the way for church reuse *Rory Quinn*
The use and abuse of church 're-use': a historical perspective from 1833 to the present *Steven Saxby*
Historic churches: heritage and voluntary action *Robert Piggott*
Working cooperatively with closed churches: the Holland Coastal Group *Stella Jackson*
What is the future for historic parish churches? *Peter Aiers*

Published September 2016.

William Stephen Gilly
An exceptionally busy life

Hugh Norwood
Edited and completed by **Nicholas Groves**

The life of W. S. Gilly (1789–1855) was remarkable in its depth and breadth of achievement – as preacher, writer, social reformer and philanthropist.

Gilly was born in Suffolk. After studying at Christ's Hospital, he lambasted the public school system. As a young clergyman in East London he preached to an inattentive Charles Dickens. The main path of his life was set by two events: his second marriage to a rich woman and his visit to the valleys in Piedmont where Waldensian Protestants had settled.

Gilly spearheaded English attempts to help the Waldensians, and as prebend of Durham Cathedral and vicar of Norham, in the Borders, he also became a notable agitator for social reform in the North-East, working for the poor of Durham and the hinds, the travelling Border labourers.

272 pp, with 42 b/w illustrations including sketches of Piedmont by Gilly's wife Jane, and 6 maps.

Hugh Norwood *studied economics and history at Bristol University, becoming a town planner and later an author and publisher. The book was completed after his death by* **Nicholas Groves**.

For details of hard copy and electronic editions of titles published by the Lasse Press, visit:

www.lassepress.com